ACID
ATTACK

A JOURNALIST'S
WAR WITH
ORGANISED CRIME

ACID ATTACK

A JOURNALIST'S WAR WITH ORGANISED CRIME

RUSSELL FINDLAY

BIRLINN

First published in 2018 by
Birlinn Limited
West Newington House
10 Newington Road
Edinburgh
EH9 1QS

www.birlinn.co.uk

ISBN: 978 1 78027 499 7

British Library Cataloguing-in-Publication Data
A catalogue record for this book is available from the British Library

Typeset by Initial Typesetting Services, Edinburgh
Printed and bound by MBM Print SCS Ltd, East Kilbride

To my family and friends,
thank you for loving and listening

To those who share their stories,
your trust is an immense privilege

And to all reporters and photographers,
don't ever back down

CONTENTS

1

SPECIAL DELIVERY

Two days before Christmas and the red blur of a postman's jacket could be seen through the frosted glass of my front door. I eased it open slightly and his hand passed through a Royal Mail card and pen, with a mumbled instruction to sign for an unexpected special delivery. As I turned slightly to my left and looked down to scrawl my name, a shock of cold liquid splashed upwards across my face. From my mouth came a scream of terror. A glass bottle flew past my head. Mere milliseconds had passed but my brain calmly informed me that I was under attack – that some kind of toxic liquid had been thrown in my face and that my life was in danger.

The postman was fake. The card a distraction. His special delivery, I later learned, was a bottle of sulphuric acid. His task was to blind and maim – possibly even murder.

The empty bottle was instantly followed by the postman himself, who crashed into the hallway and lunged towards me. Fight or flight? repel him and retreat? or meet force with force? Truth is, there was no such choice. I had to get the postman out of my home, where I lived alone with my 10-year-old daughter, who was enjoying a long lie on the first day of the school holidays. With all my strength, I expelled him back into the cold morning air. We fell out through the door in an unorthodox embrace. We tripped, pirouetted and I landed on my back. A rib cracked as the postman's bulk collapsed on top of me, forcing the air from my lungs.

My face was burning and the skin felt tight. The taste in my mouth was foul and bitter. My right eye – doused in acid – gave the ordinary suburban street a soft white filter, as if it were a dream. I sank my teeth into his meaty head and frantically gouged at his face and eyes, TV having taught me the importance of getting his DNA under my nails. The postman scrambled to his feet and lumbered towards the road. 'YOU'RE GOING FUCKING NOWHERE,' I bellowed, grabbing desperately at his Royal Mail jacket, which came away in my hands like a snake's skin. He broke free, lurching towards his idling getaway car, but he was too slow and my fingers just managed to regain their grip. We both crashed back down hard onto the monoblock driveway, where we flailed violently. I was wrestling for control – he was fighting to flee. The tables turned. I was now on top of the postman. The getaway driver panicked and drove off, leaving him stranded. I straddled the expanse of his stomach and jabbed him with my fist, hard on the face.

Over my shoulder, I saw my daughter in pyjama shorts and T-shirt, wide-eyed and frozen. Having heard the doorbell, she had crept out of bed and edged curiously to the top of the stairs to see who was calling – perhaps a friend with an early Christmas gift. Clasping her favourite stuffed toy to her chest, her face was a study of fear and confusion as her mind tried to make sense of this extraordinary scene. Her piercing cry of 'DAD!' struck at my heart. I shouted at her to go to a nearby friend's house. 'Run, quickly!' She didn't pause. Springing out of the doorway, her little bare feet almost tripped over the postman's boots as she bravely dashed a couple of doors along, fearful that he would give chase to stop her.

She hammered the door and our friend, a lady in her sixties, opened it to the sight of a tearful and terrified little girl, her urgent plea for help so garbled as to be almost incoherent. The startled neighbour then saw me on top of a postman and I shouted that I had been attacked. I urged her to get the police and ambulance. She phoned 999 and shepherded my daughter inside to safety, where she curled up beside our friend's pet dogs, who comforted her with gentle familiarity and warmth.

It was just past 8.30 a.m. and I was wearing only a pair of pyjama bottoms and grey T-shirt. My bare feet were bruised and shredded by the brick driveway but the adrenaline masked any pain.

Having gained the upper hand and by now utterly consumed by rage and indignation, I took the opportunity to pause, to catch my breath and to examine my attacker. With my teeth set in a clench of anger, I grinned manically at the despicable thug trapped beneath me. As I stared into his piggy eyes, the only emotion on show was bewilderment. This was clearly not how he had seen his day unfolding. He had come to my home to inflict serious damage but had instead become my captive, now as helpless as a beached jellyfish.

I hammered my fist so hard into his face that his set of dentures flew out of his mouth and broke in two. With an amusing lack of self-awareness, he wailed, 'MY TEETH!' Each punch was joyful and satisfactory, instant doses of justice. My only later regret was that I showed too much restraint. More appropriate perhaps would have been to dispense biblical redress by taking his sight as he had intended to take mine – an eye for an eye.

'What's your name?' I asked but he was mute. His fight

was mostly gone and all he could do was to gob bloody chunks of phlegm at me, which ceased when I recipro-cated with a foaming white blob of acidic spit. By now, the street was slowly filling with residents edging out of front doors – good people whose faces were etched with concern and disbelief. This quiet enclave – a haven where children play safely, litter is absent, smiles are exchanged and neighbourly bonds still matter – had seen nothing like it. One neighbour thought that I had caught a burglar and cautioned me to ease off on the punching. I barked at him to go into my house and fetch a basin of water to rinse my face and eye. The vision in my right eye was virtually gone – everyday fine details and vivid colours had been replaced by fuzzy shapes, soft pastel tones and a hazy light.

The husband of the lady who called 999 was first at my side. He crouched beside the postman, took his wrists and pinned his arms to the ground. With my free hands, I scooped handfuls of icy water on to my face, desperately trying to wash away or dilute the cloying liquid which was eating my skin and stealing my sight. One neighbour threw the entire basin over my head, which also drenched the postman underneath me, causing him to recoil ridicu-lously in apparent umbrage. Another basin was filled and the rinsing continued. I could feel the burning sensation sink deeper as the acid intruded behind the orb of my eyeball. I gargled the water to try and clear the bitter phlegm seeping down my throat.

We maintained this position for at least 10 minutes but it felt much longer as I continually shouted for police and medical help. I fired questions at the postman – 'What's your name?', 'Who sent you?', 'Where are you from?' and 'How much were you paid?' In response, he offered either silence or glib replies such as, 'I don't know what you're talking about,' 'I'm just a postman,' and 'You just attacked me.' Occasional blows and threatened ones caused him to flinch but not loosen his tongue. This was clearly a man familiar with the criminal's right of silence. His answers were rendered even more absurd by his whiny and petulant tone, like a toddler protesting innocence despite being caught scribbling on a wall. This was no child or even a youth but a man in his fifties – a lump of grey flesh, the product of a tragic lifetime of poor diet, idleness and incarceration. I viewed him with pure contempt.

My knees were pressed firmly on his upper arms. On one arm was the tattooed name of Dominique while the other said Lorraine, both in a calligraphy-style script. The tattoos suggested the postman possessed a streak of human decency, but this was at odds with the commission of such a vile and craven act. I asked who these women were – wife? partner? daughter? – and taunted him by suggesting I should pay them a visit later when he would be locked in a police cell.

My most important question was 'What did you throw in my face?' He offered nothing but feigned ignorance. I added, 'You'd better tell me – if I end up blind, I will fucking kill you!' but he was in no mood to talk and no amount of threats or blows elicited an answer. All he could do was hold out and pray for the police to rescue him. At one point in the interrogation, I mockingly – albeit sincerely – asked, 'Why the fuck did they send a fat clown like you? Is that really all I'm worth?' The playground barbs may have hurt more than his superficial cuts and bruises.

I must have looked deranged. Dressed in pyjama bottoms on a cold winter morning, face and eye livid and ugly, sitting on top of a postman while bombarding him with questions, insults and punches.

Eventually, two figures clad in black and neon yellow ran from a police car, its blue lights and sirens adding to the madness that had shattered the pre-Christmas peace. Just as the police officers were approaching, the postman snarled, 'Wee Jamie sends his regards.' Who was Jamie? I knew of at least two major criminals of that name. But the postman refused to say any more and was hoisted to his feet and escorted to the safety of a police van which had also appeared, soon to be joined by many more blue lights, reporters, press photographers, well-wishers and gawkers who found a reason to take a drive down a cul-de-sac. Left at the scene were his snapped dentures in a pool of blood and a genuine Royal Mail bag that matched the jacket and delivery card, all of which had to be bagged as evidence and forensically examined.

One of the young police officers asked me to talk him through exactly what had happened. It was only when I reached my front door that I saw the glint of a steak knife – a black handle with six inches of sharp, serrated steel – lying across the threshold. I suddenly realised that the pristine blade had been meant for me. If the postman had done his job properly, it would have been buried in my guts and I could now be dead. At the moment he came through my door, he had lost control of his weapon. It seems that he had just too many items to carry – acid bottle, pen, delivery card, knife. It certainly didn't feel like it but it was my lucky day.

I benefited from another piece of good fortune. Less then a month prior to the attack, in December 2015, my old solid wooden front door had been replaced. Had the old door still been in use I would have seen a 'postman' through the peephole and opened it fully, exposing *both* eyes to the acid and offering a bigger target for the blade. Because I had only been able to see the blur of a red jacket through the new PVC front door's frosted glass panels, I had opened it cautiously and only partially, which had narrowed his window of attack. The stark reality is that my daughter could have come downstairs to a very different scenario – a dark outcome which is hard even to think about.

The sight and significance of the knife caused me to flip. I have never before experienced such pure and potent anger. At that moment I could have been capable of killing the postman, making me appreciate how some good people can end up in prison. Had I seen the knife sooner, as we struggled, would it have ended up inside him? I think it is possible.

I turned back towards the police van, determined to drag the postman out by his head and rip him to pieces. Black uniforms swarmed around me, forming a barrier. One police officer said, 'Calm down. You need to get to hospital – the ambulance is on its way.'

2

#FAIL

The ambulance screamed and weaved through rush-hour traffic to reach A&E in just six minutes while I lay in the back having saline water poured into my right eye and splashed over my face.

I told the paramedic what had happened. Luckily, I was not being treated for a knife wound or lying lifeless in the back of a different kind of ambulance – the discreet vans used by undertakers.

As a 42-year-old journalist I had spent years investigating organised crime. This appeared to be payback. I did not yet know who the postman was but it seemed likely he was just a hired hand, a 'rocket', paid to do the dirty work of someone with deep pockets and a deep grudge. Scotland's criminal underworld is inhabited by inadequate, thin-skinned little men who grow rich and crave status through cowardly violence, drug-dealing and the exploitation of the weakest and most vulnerable souls in society. They hate the truth being told about them. I am universally despised by them, which is just as it should be and just the way I like it.

The adrenaline was fading and my injuries were beginning to sting. My eye burned furiously and my skin was on fire. The snapped rib was making itself felt. Pain pulsed from cuts and grazes all over my body.

Shielded by police officers, I was ordered to lie back as the trolley was clattered out of the ambulance and spirited into the cavernous emergency room of Queen Elizabeth University Hospital, where a team of medics in pale blue tunics got to work. A small plastic device was attached directly to my acid-soaked eyeball which allowed sterile water to flow directly on to it – intrusive and unnatural but as welcome as a cool spring fountain on a hot summer day. I fought the instinct to flinch, blink and recoil as my precious sight was at stake. A female A&E doctor gazed into my eyes, inches from my face, and asked, 'Can you see how beautiful I am?' The answer was a wavering and bemused 'Yes,' as my right eye's vision was milky and unclear.

Five litres of water later, I was allowed to sit up. I grabbed my phone and, with two police officers in pursuit, barged through the swing doors into a public area to get a signal. Dispensing with phone etiquette, I delivered a rapid-fire account of what had happened to an agog reporter at *The Scottish Sun*, where I was the Investigations Editor. I told her about the postman's 'Wee Jamie' remark and speculated that the two most likely candidates were Jamie Daniel and Jamie Stevenson, high-level organised criminals I had pursued in newspapers and books.

Daniel – who was to die of natural causes six months after my attack – was head of his eponymous family gang which spread from Glasgow's deprived Possil area to forge links with major UK and international criminal networks. They stayed anonymous for years until my colleagues and I decided to shine a light on their drug-dealing, murdering and money-laundering. The family's war with the Lyons gang, which continues to rage after more than 17 years, was the subject of my book *Caught in the Crossfire*, published in 2012.

Stevenson was also from north Glasgow and subject of another book – *The Iceman* – which I co-wrote in 2008. Taking its title from one of Stevenson's nicknames, it tells how he quietly became one of Scotland's most active narcotics smugglers until he was jailed for money-laundering. Stevenson was prime suspect in the fatal shooting of his former best friend, drug-dealer Tony McGovern, in 2000, a murder which remains unsolved.

Call finished, I was met outside A&E by a friend and newspaper colleague. I retold the story but this time my emotions kicked in. Angry tears spilled down my cheeks and my voice cracked as I described how the fake postman had come to my home with absolutely no regard for the safety of my 10-year-old daughter. Even by the low standards of the criminal world, it was contemptible. Next time some washed-up old gangster opines about an underworld code of honour, about 'non-combatants' and children being exempt from violence, just remember that it is a myth, invented as a means of trying to justify the unjustifiable and give a veneer of legitimacy to the illegitimate.

I was discharged from A&E and pushed in a wheelchair through the hospital. With my police guards, I raised eyebrows as we whizzed through waiting areas and eventually found the ophthalmology department, where experts puzzled over what liquid had been used by the postman. More water was flushed through the damaged cornea and the first of many batches of eye drops was issued. Over the following weeks, putting in drops became a full-time occupation. There was Hylo-Forte (16 per day); Dropodex (9 per day); Minims Chloramphenicol 0.5% (4 per day); Cyclopentolate Hydrochloride 1% (1 per day); Xailin (night-time). The ophthalmologist's prognosis was cautious and mixed. I had scarring on my right cornea and there was a chance the sight could deteriorate until it was gone for good. The harsh news was softened by the overriding caveat that it was too early to know.

I was then taken by police car to another hospital, the Royal Infirmary, where a consultant plastic surgeon examined the chemical burns on my face. After leaving the second hospital, my phone came alive with missed calls, messages, voicemails and emails from friends, relatives and colleagues as news of the attack spread through newspaper offices and beyond. It was impossible to address them all at once. Sitting in the front passenger seat of a marked police car, I used Twitter to compose a succinct message of defiance: 'Fat hitman left his teeth in my driveway #fail.' I figured that people would deduce that if I was well enough to tweet, my injuries were not life-threatening. It served another purpose and that was to tell the postman's paymasters that their plot to have me stuck like a pig had gone badly wrong. The getaway driver would have already confessed to abandoning the postman. The tweet rubbed it right in. A friend cautioned against it as it could inflame the situation or be twisted and used against me later by a defence lawyer, but I rejected the advice because I wanted people to know that I was fine and had come out on top. If defiance was mistaken for gloating, so be it.

It was early afternoon when I arrived back home in the police car, but it felt already like one of the longest days of my life. The circus had been and gone, the police tape removed. Neighbours told how the street had been filled with blue-light vehicles, including fire engines due to the use of a chemical substance. One mum who popped out for her Christmas turkey before the attack was unable to get home as the street was in lockdown.

Stepping through the front door, the attack felt distant and unreal, as if it had all been imagined. Then I saw the hallway's freshly painted white walls streaked with the viscous brown fluid which had been thrown upwards into my face from close range. The powerful acid was eating into the plaster and corroding the enamel paint on the radiator. Drops of it defaced the glass surface of a mirror and permanently marked a wooden table. Also splattered was a festive holly wreath set for the front door, and a singing Christmas tree. Drops of acid were dotted on my daughter's shoes. These and other items were bagged and binned. It would take more than six coats of white emulsion to finally obliterate all traces of acid from the walls.

I returned to the police car which took me to Partick police station, where the CID were waiting for a statement. Sitting in a drab little room, I recounted the day's events in painstaking, chronological detail. When it came to the question of whether I had seen the knife in the postman's hand, there were two ways of answering. I could have said yes, knowing that this might help bolster the police and prosecution case. But that answer would have been untrue. To lie would be foolish as it would serve only to help the postman by giving his lawyer something to unpick and challenge – ammunition to cast doubt on my evidence. Anyway, such embellishment was unnecessary as the postman had been caught at the scene of the crime, in a fancy-dress costume, and the police had numerous independent and credible witnesses. The only thing that would make his prosecution more of a gift would have been for me to wrap him in Christmas paper, stick a bow on his head and leave him under the tree.

More than an hour into the interminable interview, I found my concentration beginning to lapse. I realised that I had not eaten a single thing since waking. The incredible day had been fuelled entirely on adrenaline and one cup of tea, which I had been drinking in bed while reading on my Kindle when the postman rang. Having awoken before 8 a.m., it was now around 3 p.m. I could hardly think straight. A jarring thought occurred – the postman would, no doubt, have had a nice hot lunch, courtesy of the police. They know their rights. A CID officer went to fetch me one of the most satisfying meals I have ever experienced – a can of Diet Coke, a bag of crisps and a Bounty bar. Having devoured them, I got back on track to finish the statement.

When I finally got home, the house was dark, silent and cold. Unable to drive because of my injured eye, a friend took me to another house where my daughter was and it was deemed sensible to spend the night. A storm raged outside as I lay awake until the early hours, exhausted but unable to switch off my racing thoughts.

One of my daughter's favourite Christmas movies is *Home Alone*, in which two bungling criminals are carted off by the police. That our Christmas scrape had a similar Hollywood-style ending with the postman locked up made my job of reassuring her that all was well much easier. It would have been a hard task if the postman had still been at large. What would that uncertainty have done to a child? Even worse was the thought of him managing to use his knife on me.

The overwhelming torrent of messages intensified, arriving more quickly than they could be responded to. That evening I needed to get out to clear my head. I stood alone in an unfamiliar pub in an unfamiliar town. Other patrons presumably gave me a wide berth – an odd stranger, face covered with scarlet patches and one puffy red eye virtually swollen shut.

I thought deeply about who might have ordered such an audacious, extraordinary and carefully planned attack

3

BASIL FAULTY

William Burns stood handcuffed and silent in the familiar comfort of a court dock with his bowed head resembling a misshapen lump of raw steak mince. Much of his existence has been spent in prison cells due to an unfortunate and unshakeable habit of dealing drugs, waving guns around and, on at least one occasion, shooting people.

The court heard that Burns was charged with assaulting me by pretending to be a postman and throwing sulphuric acid in my face. As Burns slouched in the dock, his name came to me by text. It chimed but vaguely. He had never merited significant journalistic attention, largely due to his being off the radar through spells in prison. Brief proceedings over, Burns was carted off to jail, where he would awaken the next morning – Christmas Day – without so much as a selection box. Perhaps his HMP Barlinnie brethren had a whip round for a 55th birthday gift two days later. Bail was not on the agenda because Burns had been out on licence when he attacked me, having been released early from a prison sentence for the shooting of an unarmed female security guard, who had only been trying to do her job. He fired a pistol at her from point-blank range during a Post Office robbery which netted him the princely sum of £15,500. Thankfully, his innocent victim survived. For that, a judge called Lord Penrose sentenced Burns to 15 years in prison but, this being Scotland, it could mean just about anything.

The Crown Office and judiciary make loud noises when lengthy sentences are imposed on bad men. These are hailed unquestioningly on TV news, but many people have grown astute enough to know these numbers are virtually meaningless. The reality is that the length of time served is typically a fraction of what is stated. Clarity only applies to life sentences for which judges are required to set a minimum prison term. Not only are the lengths of sentences a sham, the public have no right to know when criminals are freed. Nor are they entitled to know if and when they are sent back to prison for breaching early release terms. All of these decisions are made behind closed doors by the Parole Board for Scotland.

Burns is a classic case in point of dishonest and secretive sentencing. Despite being jailed for 15 years in 2001, it was decided to put him back on the streets of Paisley after 10 years. We only know this because he became involved in a violent feud – stabbings all round – with a drug-dealing murderer and former crony called Stewart Gillespie. It was decided, again entirely in secret, that both Burns and Gillespie should be sent back to jail to serve the rest of their respective prison sentences. This hokey-cokey routine only reached the public domain thanks to journalist Derek Alexander, whose underworld contacts are unmatched. It was his story that alerted the shooting victim that Burns had even been freed in the first place.

The secret decision to return Burns to prison was clearly sensible. The only problem being, it was again decreed – yes, in secret – that Burns should be let out early for a *second* time. We only know this because I sat on him in my driveway in December 2015 when he was supposedly serving the 15-year sentence which should have run until July 2016.

Burns first came to public attention in 1994 as a participant in a drugs war that poisoned the proud town of Paisley and its bordering south Glasgow housing estates of Nitshill and Pollok. He was in a craven gang controlled by a man called Stewart 'Specky' Boyd. The gang was linked to at least nine murders, most of them still unsolved. They were the closest that Scotland has ever had to the cartels of Mexico and Colombia, where killing is done on an industrial scale. One wonders what the body count would have been had they not been impeded by our strict gun laws.

The 1990s Paisley drugs war didn't receive anything like the media scrutiny it merited at the time. Most of the attention was focused on the then Paisley North MP Irene Adams, who suffered death threats for speaking out against the mob. The Labour politician's sister, who died of a suspected drugs overdose in 2001, had two children with the brother of Burns.

Other prominent members of the gang included Gillespie, Robert 'Piggy' Pickett and George 'Goofy' Docherty. Dumb nicknames appear to be coincidental not conditional. Burns also has one – Basil. This came not from any fondness of the fragrant herb nor the madcap hotelier of 1970s sitcom *Fawlty Towers* nor, sadly, the kids' TV fox Basil Brush with the 'Boom Boom!' catchphrase. Rather, Basil was a violent old crook who Burns idolised to the extent that he took his name as a nickname, like a rock band tribute act.

In 1994 Burns stood trial for the fatal shooting of another rival dealer called Raymond McCafferty in Glasgow – a kneecapping gone wrong, apparently – but was cleared. The police firmly believe that Burns got away with murder. A relative of the murdered man declined my offer to talk. Underworld sources suggest Burns got paid just £2,000 for the 'job'.

Two years later, in August 1996, a different jury found Burns guilty of stealing a *Lion King* birthday cake from a Marks & Spencer store . . . at gunpoint. When a security guard caught Burns trying to purloin the novelty Disney confection in November 1994, he stuck a Browning 9mm handgun in his face, threatened to shoot him and then ran away.

Police and prosecutors signally failed to deal with this toxic quintet during their long and depraved reign of murder and mayhem in Paisley. The people of the town and surrounding areas were let down badly. The lack of a media spotlight almost certainly contributed to the police and Crown's indifference.

Natural selection and street justice eventually did the authorities' job for them. Boyd died in a car crash in Spain in 2003. Tragically, five innocent lives were also lost. Docherty was run over and stabbed to death in Glasgow in 2006. His murder is unsolved. Pickett was shot in Glasgow in 2006 but survived. He still skulks around Paisley and is a close ally of Burns. Gillespie was stabbed to death in Paisley in 2013. His killer was jailed. Burns is due to spend at least the next few years in prison and will be a spent force once released. Other than throwing acid, shooting an innocent woman and the birthday cake heist, he has convictions involving assault, robbery, guns, knives and bail breach. As one of life's great leeches, goodness knows what the cost, borne by society, must be for his prison time and legal aid lawyers.

Once I learned of his identity, I hoped that it would become the first piece of a jigsaw which would eventually build a clear picture of the entire attack plot and everyone involved in it. But something was not right. In the hours after the attack, amidst the whirlwind of police officers and medics, I believed it most likely emanated from the Daniel mob, in part due to the snarled parting shot that 'Wee Jamie sends his regards'. I had quickly discounted the paymaster being Jamie Stevenson, aka 'The Iceman', partly because he is a big man who Burns would not describe as 'wee'. Furthermore, despite his presumed animus towards me, I doubted that Stevenson would be so reckless as to target a journalist because of the serious heat and backlash it could generate.

In the days before the attack, I had been working on an investigation centred on the Daniels. A family member was suspected of deliberately driving a car at Roy Wolfin, a multimillionaire with interests in private hire taxis, property and payday loans, and a known associate of the Daniels. It did not appear to be the driver's intention but Wolfin lost both his legs in the sickening hit-and-run. My story about this was published on 20 December, three days before the acid attack. But now, on hearing that Burns was in the dock, the immediate Daniel theory made no sense whatsoever. Burns and his close friend Pickett are closely allied to the Lyons gang who, in turn, are both sworn enemies of the Daniel mob.

My book *Caught in the Crossfire* charts how the Lyons and Pickett's Paisley contingent joined forces to fight the Daniels, on the basis of 'my enemy's enemy is my friend'. The 2006 shooting of Pickett was carried out by two Daniel hitmen, using stolen British army guns. In that Daniel atrocity, one Lyons family member was killed and another was wounded.

The only conclusion was that the 'Wee Jamie' comment had been a deliberate act of misinformation from Burns – a smokescreen to temporarily confuse me and send me in the wrong direction, which it did.

Another aspect of the attack was beginning to take on growing significance. Scanning through old newspaper cuttings, I saw that Burns had spent a lifetime using guns on people. That was his comfort zone. Yet he came to my door wielding a bottle of acid. The intent of his paymaster was to destroy my face, to blind me, disfigure me, maim me for life. Just type 'acid attack' into Google Images for a graphic depiction of what they were hoping for me.

Puzzled London journalist Andy Lines, chief reporter of the *Daily Mirror*, asked a Glasgow colleague, 'Why didn't 'e just shoot 'im?' A gun would have denoted business. Acid was personal. It was not the Daniel mob, so who was it? My suspicions were growing, but I was keeping an open mind.

4

GET A HAIRCUT

The year after William 'Basil' Burns committed his birth-day-cake heist, I was offered my first job as a journalist.

Peering through thick glasses across a vast expanse of desk, *Daily Record* editor-in-chief Endell Laird told me in clipped tones the annual salary was £9,500 and that my hair was too long – welcome aboard but get a haircut. My flowing golden locks, a legacy of a summer job in a Californian fairground, did not impress the traditional newspaper man, but he was willing to take a chance on me not being a moron. Aged 20, I felt like a big shot landing the job of reporter at *The Glaswegian*, a bright and punchy but now defunct free title which was then delivered to most homes in the city. Although quite how many ended up turning the River Clyde into papier mâché will never be known.

From childhood, I only ever wanted to be a journalist. Sitting at the kitchen table, I devoured newspapers with an insatiable zeal. As a teenage schoolboy, I made myself busy at the suburban local paper with work experience and unpaid rugby and football match reports. I quit school halfway through sixth year, figuring I needed experience rather than qualifications, and took a job in a petrol station while trying to learn about my intended profession. Stuart Barr, a veteran *Daily Record* journalist who lived nearby, kindly agreed to give me a grounding in the basics. Off we went to cover junior football for the *Evening Times*. Having just 60 words to describe the bloodshed and drama of a typical clash – fists and feet flying, red cards, crowd trouble, a 5–4 scoreline – was great discipline. When I proudly acquired my first press card, it showed an 18-year-old with floppy hair.

Sport had been my only real interest at school but I managed to scrape a B in Higher English to study journalism at Napier University in Edinburgh, where shorthand was by far the most useful lesson. Student life gave me a brief foray into politics. Using the *nom de guerre* Dr Freelove and Lager, I stood for student union president, to the disgust of genuine candidates. I hastily withdrew after early voting suggested I was romping towards an unwanted victory.

At *The Glaswegian* I was expected to do every job and filled countless empty white boxes with news and sports exclusives, lifestyle features, motors and even movie reviews (quite a feat without having seen the films). One insightful job was typing up a freelance's nuggets of scandal and gossip from the Labour-dominated council. 'The Backbencher' column's tales of back-stabbing, bullying and bungs were a prime example of journalism being the telling of stories that some people didn't want told. In an ever-changing world, it has provided some comfort that the 'cooncil' has so valiantly preserved its proud tradition of sleaze and corruption.

A colleague, a member of the Catholic Church's strict Opus Dei sect, caused mirth with a weekly act of sabotage – jumbling up the star signs before they were published. So an unwitting Aries would end up reading the Virgo horoscope. It was a one-man stand against astrology.

With an empty back page to fill, the boss dispatched me

to Celtic Park to ask captain Paul McStay about the likelihood of a testimonial match. Unimpressed by my line of questioning, the veteran footballer sent me packing. Later that day McStay phoned the office to apologise to me – a mere green young hack – for his offhand demeanour. It was an astonishing act of courtesy from a decent man.

I sourced two police scandals that were pinched by the national press. One was about an Asian officer who suffered racist bullying by colleagues and the other was about sexism inflicted on a female officer. These would not be my last clashes with irate police chiefs. Despite a middle-class upbringing, I had developed a healthy suspicion of the police. When I was 17, the son of a high-ranking police chief hurled a brick through my windscreen as I drove under a pedestrian bridge. He and his pals had spent months antagonising my friends and me. Hidden hands got to work. To my astonishment, a few days later, two police officers turned up at the petrol station where I worked and publicly charged me with chasing the brick-thrower many months earlier. Yes, I had pursued him one night after he had shouted threats at me but he got away. It was a complete non-incident but enough to dig out and use as a counterweight against the brick-throwing, which could have killed me. Both cases entered the opaque corridors of the Crown Office and disappeared.

My biggest story at *The Glaswegian* was an undercover sting. A housing official entrusted to distribute European Union beef to poor residents of Anderston was flogging it on the side. Once I'd handed over £100 for an illicit consignment of 1,200 tins, I revealed my identity to the rogue, who promptly did a runner only to be later convicted in court. It was the first and only time I allowed my photo to be published – poker-faced in the back of a Ford Transit, holding aloft contraband meat.

Another undercover foray was to buy a 'snuff' movie from the Barras market, long before Islamist terrorists honed the genre and turned it mainstream. With great anticipation, the VHS tape was slid into the office machine but the grainy footage looked suspiciously like something from a B-movie horror flick.

I learned that a journalist is nothing without contacts who are willing to share tips and information. It takes years to acquire them. They often take great risks in speaking. Forget chequebook journalism – trust is the only currency that matters.

One journalistic maxim is that you should never become the story. It's a rule that I tried to stick to for more than 20 years, but the acid attack put paid to that. It was unsettling and surreal to see my name all over newspapers' lurid accounts of a botched gangland hit and the more formal reports of Burns' court appearance. Relatives on holiday in Norway even heard of the attack while listening to BBC Radio 2's breakfast news. My boss, Gordon Smart, then editor of *The Scottish Sun* where I worked, was quoted as saying, 'Russell is a brilliant and fearless reporter.' His comments would later take on a bitter significance.

Once it had been on the evening TV news and spread online, it seemed that everybody I have ever known in my entire life got in touch with me. A thoughtful email arrived from Lesley Thomson, who was then the Solicitor General, Scotland's second most senior prosecutor. Thomson, who I had met professionally on no more than a few occasions, said, 'I know this won't stop your investigative work on organised crime groups!' Another came from Graeme Pearson, a former senior police officer turned Labour MSP, who said, 'Sorry to hear you were attacked on your doorstep. Looks as though you gave a good account of yourself and I am glad you got an arrest out of it too!'

Word also reached me from a criminal asking if it would be possible to acquire Burns' broken false teeth so that they could be worn as a necklace. Was he joking? The teeth were in a police evidence bag, but I was not convinced that a bloody set of dentures would have the same vibe as the shark's fang worn round Crocodile Dundee's neck. Another made an apparently serious proposal through a third party to buy me a bottle of Bollinger champagne as a 'thank you' on behalf of Burns's appreciative victims. I politely declined.

The outpouring of kind words, especially from establishment figures, was disconcerting – much like being a guest at my own funeral. One close friend texted to say he was 'really proud' of me, but a few weeks later, deploying the acerbic humour of newspaper hacks, came this fantastic and unforgettable put-down: 'Just cos you've battered a fat junkie before he gets his morning dose of methadone you think you're chocolate.'

The wide-eyed and fresh-faced young hack who walked out of the imposing old landmark *Daily Record* building in 1993 with a spring in his step and a contract in his hands had no idea that, almost a quarter of a century later, he would be making the news and for all the wrong reasons.

5

LIZARD'S TAIL

The torrent of goodwill towards me was humbling and appreciated, but of greater interest regarding the acid attack itself were the tantalising pearls of intelligence about the identity of the postman's puppet-master.

William 'Basil' Burns is dangerous and amoral, as evidenced by his lengthy, tawdry history and willingness to stab and throw acid into a journalist's face at a family home. It was clear that a great deal of effort had gone into planning the job – the establishment of my address, the certainty that I was home at the time, a trustworthy getaway driver, the creation of an exit strategy and the acquisition of Royal Mail accoutrements to pass unnoticed all point to a level of sophistication beyond that of a low-IQ thug.

When North Korean despot Kim Jong-un sent two women to assassinate his half-brother by wiping a nerve agent in his face at a Malaysian airport, they were described as 'lizard's tails'. Burns was dressed as a postie and one Pyongyang killer wore a T-shirt with LOL on it, but what they had in common other than memorable outfits and targeting of faces with dangerous substances was that they were expendable assets. Like a lizard losing its tail in a scrape, the arrest of Burns was no more than an inconvenience to his paymaster. He was completely disposable.

He may not even realise that prison is full of throwaway Basils, used and discarded just like him. Burns has spent a lifetime demonstrating that he does not possess the inclination or basic skills required to regret, reform, rebuild or make a contribution to society. Common decency is an alien concept. The tragic truth, which he may know deep down, is that he prefers the comfort blanket of incarceration – a self-centred existence of structure and routine, no bills, fully catered for, free clothing and zero pressure to work, adapt, provide or prosper. In prison he enjoys a perverse kudos from the notoriety of his Paisley gang.

The person or people who wound him up, stuffed a fat wad of Christmas cash into his hand and sent him to my door were confident that his arrest posed no meaningful threat to them. When Burns sat down to be interviewed by the CID, his boss or bosses would have been confident that the only words to pass from his mouth would be: 'No comment.' Of that, they were proved entirely correct.

Winston Churchill once said: 'You have enemies? Good. That means you've stood up for something, sometime in your life.' Having poked and prodded Scotland's major organised criminals for many years, I have no shortage of them. I did not go seeking them but, in my view, such people are worthwhile enemies to have. I've often said that life is not a popularity contest. To borrow another classic quote, supposedly from Oscar Wilde: 'You can always judge a man by the quality of his enemies.'

Tom Minogue, a retired self-made businessman and blogger from Fife, a man never afraid to ruffle establishment feathers, tweeted this take hours after the acid attack: 'Russell has taken on Glasgow gangsters, crooked cops, bent politicians, judges, lawyers ... pretty much everyone. Take your pick!' I couldn't have put it better myself.

Trying to ascertain who had directed the attack was similar to working on any other news story, the unique and jarring difference being that I was the subject of my own enquiries. Burns was the lizard's tail, but who was the lizard? I had already established, contrary to early clues, that it had *not* been ordered by the Daniel gang. But who was the man, or men, with the resources – intelligence, guile, cash – to plan such an unusual job? Which gangland thug, or thugs, had been so riled by the truth being written about them that they would resort to an acid attack?

Trusted contacts got in touch to offer nuggets of intelligence, to be considered and cross-referenced with other information coming in from different sources. Journalists at the newspaper where I worked and friends on other papers were united in disgust. Newspaper journalists often have a quicker and clearer handle on gangland intelligence than the police. They made it their business to go fishing for answers. One excitedly trumpeted to his colleagues: 'We need to find out who sent Basil Fawlty!' Another added, rather unhelpfully: 'Every gangster in Scotland would have chipped in to get you done in.' No doubt, many of the killers, drug-dealers, paedophiles, money launderers, crooked lawyers and street thugs would have taken some pleasure from what had befallen me. But some criminals I had exposed were horrified, recognising that such a vile attack was unjustifiable.

Like a breakthrough moment in a major police enquiry, one phone call provided me with at least some of the answers. I was not in the least surprised at the name imparted to me, but one of the reasons offered to justify the attack was a bombshell. The caller told me, 'It came from Donuts. He already hates you because of the stories you've done about him. But he's now been telling people that you're in a relationship with his ex.'

Frankie 'Donuts' Donaldson was a name I knew well and a man I was wary of. He is at the pinnacle of organised crime in Scotland. He is too cunning, cowardly or clever to confront his enemies face to face. He saves his own explosive violence for women. He has accrued a personal fortune estimated at many millions of pounds. His jealous enemies suspect he has thrived due to being far too close to some in the police. He detests any kind of press scrutiny. He has expressed a furious dislike at the attention I have given him over many years. He courts senior members of the legal establishment, including a lawyer nicknamed 'Big Invoice' for his love of under-the-table cash. One of his biggest gripes is the publication of his nickname – 'Donuts' – supposedly earned as a young hood when he hung around a donut stand in Calton in Glasgow's east end. Compared with 'Basil', 'Piggy', 'Goofy' and 'Specky', I don't know what he's complaining about. Most worryingly, he had previously attempted to obtain personal information about me.

Then came the bombshell. To my astonished disbelief, Donaldson had got it into his head that I was involved romantically with his former partner, Jane Clarke – a woman I have never even met. His theory was fiction. However, I knew and understood *why* he might have believed it. For around 18 months prior to the acid attack, I had been in a relationship with a woman who lived in the same block of flats as Donaldson's ex. Glasgow is the biggest city in Scotland but it can feel smaller than a village. It is almost certain that I would have been the subject of surveillance prior to the attack, in order to build up a picture of my appearance, vehicle, associates and routine. There are no shortage of private detectives, some of them ex-police officers with whiffy careers, who will take on such a job, no matter who the target is or who is paying them.

The money for their surveillance helps them to overlook the possibility of any ugly consequences. One such private detective offers another sinister service – pinpointing the exact location of anyone's mobile phone using network providers' masts. Known as 'pinging' a number, the people who pay for this illegal act are often spouses trying to catch a cheating partner. Previously a tool only available to the police and security services, it can now be deployed by any crook with a few quid. Knowing where someone is 24 hours a day can be of great benefit to criminals, who mostly operate in a constant state of twitchy, sleepless paranoia. One Glasgow drug-dealer routinely pings the numbers of his own couriers to ensure they are where they should be and not taking any unauthorised detours.

Another means of locating people's movements is through the use of small tracking devices which can be fitted to the underside of vehicles. These tiny transmitters send real-time mapping of a car's movement to an app on a mobile phone. This service is also offered by some private detectives, but the inexpensive devices can just as easily be bought online.

In the months prior to the attack, I had spent significant periods of time in the same block of flats where Donaldson's former partner lived. So, on the safe assumption that I had been targeted – whether by physical surveillance, pinging my mobile or car-tracking tech – it would have been established that I was a frequent and overnight visitor to the immediate environs of Donaldson's ex. It was a staggering coincidence and a case of two plus two equals five. As far as I was concerned, it was pretty bad luck indeed.

Other possible motives for the attack remained valid, and more would emerge. I was also yet to learn about the suggested peripheral involvement of other criminals which pointed to an element of collaboration. All this was spinning through my mind during an otherworldly Christmas period which was hectic and intense. Bouncing between medical appointments in hospitals across the city, my phone did not stop ringing and beeping with countless well-meaning people seeking updates and offering assistance. Parcels of food appeared at my front door as did hand-delivered letters of support from people I did not know.

Security measures were installed at my home. On Christmas Eve – before I learned of Burns's name – I received two phone calls from a woman asking if I was Mr Burns. It had been a police officer calling to arrange a time to install a black box which would emit a priority 999 call from my home if activated. She had mistakenly read the name of my attacker from her worksheet.

Ever present was the cold fear of not knowing whether I would lose my sight or be horrifically scarred for life. That terror was kept at bay in large part by the frantic intensity of the medical merry-go-round, the incessant phone calls and my desperate and insatiable quest for answers. I kept my fears hidden from friends and family behind a front of jokey dismissiveness and defiance, but when the lights went out at night, I could not fool myself.

On the morning of Christmas Eve, just as my attacker appeared in court, I attended the Royal Infirmary's burns unit where the long-term impact of the sulphuric acid was assessed. The entire right-hand side of my face was a dramatic splatter of red – as if it had been blasted by a shotgun. The nurse, a kind woman who had seen a hell of a lot worse, told me that its appearance would deteriorate before it would improve but it was too early to know what the long-term damage might be. The only treatment was to apply a thick smear of protective Vaseline.

From there, it was off to a police station, where my various injuries were captured as evidence by a photographer. At the police station, I first met Detective Sergeant Craig Warren, the CID officer in charge of the investigation. Many in the upper echelons of the police establishment regarded me with suspicion or hostility due to the many stories I have written about corruption, dishonesty and incompetence, but Warren seemed bright, open and professional.

That same busy day I was back at the Queen Elizabeth University Hospital, where I had been rushed to A&E the previous morning. Another ophthalmologist looked deep into the scarred cornea and made the same kind of ominous noises a plumber or mechanic uses just before you have to write a big cheque. He said that the previous day's relatively positive diagnosis had been premature. I needed to understand that my eye had suffered a severe traumatic injury and it was in a bad way. More time was needed. Immediately after hearing that news, my mask of defiance slipped during a phone call with one of my bosses in London who I have known since the day I first did work experience on my local newspaper as an eager young schoolboy. Running close to empty, I was too emotional to talk.

6

FRANKIE DONUTS

Frankie Donaldson is a criminal so thin-skinned that he once hired a QC to gag a newspaper from calling him by his nickname of 'Donuts'. He was laughed out of court and left to pay all legal costs. This anecdote may be amusing and a revealing example of ego and wealth blinding reason, but it would be a foolish mistake to regard Donaldson as a figure of fun. He has spent decades at the dark heart of Scotland's sophisticated and lucrative criminal underworld which turns over unquantifiable sums – hundreds of millions of pounds each year being a conservative guess.

While contemporaries ended up in jail or violently killed, Donaldson used his ruthlessness and cunning to stay free and prosper, quietly building an estimated multi-million-pound fortune and an international property portfolio. Not bad, given there is no obvious source for his wealth.

Over decades, he has instilled genuine fear in his rivals – despite that word becoming almost meaningless through overuse when describing the criminal fraternity. The fear is not imbued through Donaldson's willingness to personally use guns, knives or fists. He doesn't do that: that's how you end up in prison. The fear comes from his deep pockets and his skill in identifying, courting, controlling and using highly dangerous men to do his dirty work – the kind of pliable men who would throw acid in the face of a journalist, for example.

Donaldson's dislike of me germinated in 2001 with my reporting of the trial of gangster John 'Joker' McCartney, who was accused and cleared of having a 9mm Browning handgun. The police gun seizure foiled a plot to shoot Donaldson, resulting in the headline 'HITMAN PLOTTED TO PUT A HOLE IN FRANKIE THE DONUT'. Three years later, McCartney survived being shot in a Glasgow pub, the alleged gunman being a brother of Donaldson's recently deceased associate Stewart 'Specky' Boyd.

Donaldson craves respect. Journalists who do their jobs properly should never respect such people. The story annoyed Donaldson but what really riled him, apparently, was being called Frankie 'the Donut'. The 'hole-in-Donut' headline was disrespectful. You cannot square that particular circle. There was no cause to dwell on the story or realise its significance at the time, but it sowed the seeds of Donaldson's hostility towards me.

Two years after that, my then newspaper, the *Sunday Mail*, produced an investigation that attempted to measure the financial worth of the country's wealthiest criminals and it featured Donaldson. The article told that when he was jailed in the 1980s for a drugs offence, he had tried to commit suicide in Barlinnie prison. It also told how he once took out a contract on a former Rangers and Scotland footballer for the alleged indecent assault of a Donaldson relative. Donaldson was incandescent at the revelations, which were written by a colleague and not by me – and yet, perversely, he apparently felt chagrin because the paper's estimate of his wealth was too small.

The following year I received a tip-off about a non-fatal shooting. Donaldson and George 'Goofy' Docherty had got into an argument with another man in a nightclub. Docherty – of Paisley mob infamy – was Donaldson's brother-in-law, his favourite henchman and as loyal as a (very dangerous) dog. The next day the man was shot by Docherty in the city's east end but survived. A short piece duly appeared, explaining that the victim was refusing to co-operate with police. It was three months after that – and out of the blue – that Donaldson came up with the ill-judged wheeze to try and silence the *Sunday Mail*. He accused the paper, incorrectly, of making up the 'Donuts' nickname and demanded that they should be stopped from using it. It was a legal first – a gangster asking a judge to stop people calling him a silly name. It was a court, not a playground.

Donaldson claimed that he had received phone calls from a *Sunday Mail* reporter, supposedly me, asking questions about his business interests. It was a mystifying claim. These calls, if they even existed, did not come from me or any of my colleagues. The most likely explanation was that a gangland rival or mischievous police officer had used my name to wind him up. I had heard of such bogus calls being made in my name before, which was hugely worrying because it meant there might be other occasions where I had no knowledge of them. That he thought the phantom caller was me was concerning as it's bad enough when criminals take exception to things that you *are* actually responsible for. In his plea to the court, Donaldson said previous articles caused him 'distress and embarrassment'. After hearing around two hours of arguments, the sheriff took minutes to reject Donaldson's groundless case. It was a humiliation which he took badly. The resultant story, again, not written by me but a colleague, told how 'paranoid Donaldson' had failed to censor the paper.

Two years after Donaldson's hubris-driven court farce came the murder of his sister's husband, George 'Goofy' Docherty, who was run over then stabbed to death in Tollcross, Glasgow. The killer has never been caught but his identity is an open secret in the underworld, where getting away with murder is the ultimate accolade. Many years later, I exposed the suspected perpetrator as a highly dangerous hitman. For Donaldson, losing his main ally was a major blow as it made him vulnerable, and I wrote a story for the *Sunday Mail* headlined 'DONUTS: THEY'LL PUT A HOLE IN ME'. The story began: 'Mobster Frankie "Donuts" Donaldson fears for his life after one of his henchmen was murdered last week.'

But there was something else within the same story which latterly was of significant interest. It was a brief account of my first and only encounter with William 'Basil' Burns before he turned up at my front door, a decade later, dressed as a postman and wielding acid. The story stated:

> Another former ally of Docherty, William 'Basil' Burns, 44, is keeping a low profile in Perth Prison where he is serving 15 years for gunning down a female security guard.
>
> But, we can reveal, he is using a mobile phone to run a drugs operation from his cell. The *Sunday Mail* obtained the number of Burns' mobile and called him in jail on Thursday. During the 35-second late-night phone call Burns confirmed who he was but refused to talk, then hung up.
>
> When told the call was from us, he said: 'What are you phoning me for? Don't phone me again.'

The source who gave the *Sunday Mail* the mobile number used by Burns said: 'Basil uses the phone to keep in touch with his outside interests. He also uses it to discuss matters that can't be said during official prison calls, which are monitored.'

The fact Burns confirmed his identity to an unknown cold caller while using an illicit phone in prison is a pretty good indicator of his mental agility. What is remarkable is that, even following the acid attack, I had no recollection of this fleeting exchange with Burns. It was so inconsequential that I forgot all about it for more than 10 years. I only remembered it four weeks after the attack when Paul Hutcheon, the *Sunday Herald*'s tenacious Investigations Editor, discovered it in a newspaper cuttings database and told me about it. I later recovered the recording of my late-night call to Burns, which was strange to hear, knowing what happened the next time our paths crossed. He was as talkative during the phone call as he had been while lying on my driveway.

From the summary of newspaper stories published about Donaldson, it may sound like he was of particular interest to me and my colleagues, but that is not the case. He is just one of the many swaggering, self-styled 'businessmen' who taint Glasgow and who seem to think they are above the law. Writing about him is not a personal crusade but merely a journalist doing his job of informing the public about people deserving attention.

Many journalists do not attempt to expose men like Donaldson. They prefer a quiet life. It is much easier to report only on the criminals who are delivered, neatly prepacked, into their email inboxes, having been processed through the criminal justice system. The serious criminals, those who routinely beat the system, would therefore evade any public scrutiny were it not for journalists with the guts to dig deep, to join the dots, to build a case that will satisfy newspaper lawyers and allow the truth to be told.

Donaldson was the subject of five stories in a six-year period from 2001, three of which I wrote – hardly a vendetta. But that's exactly what he appeared to think. Over those years and beyond, I received occasional whispers from sources about Donaldson's deep-seated hatred of me, which grew like a weed. They did not cause me any sleepless nights but I was perplexed as to why he would take it so personally and so badly. If he possessed any self-awareness, he would have realised that his own actions were the sole cause of newspaper attention.

Donaldson, however, was more than just a typical hypersensitive hood with a bad dose of misplaced umbrage. He meant business. In 2014 a trusted colleague told me that during that period when I had written about Donaldson, a car had been set alight on his orders. The car was supposed to belong to me, but given that I knew nothing of any torching, it seems that some random and unfortunate person's vehicle was destroyed by mistake. Given the sparsity of detail, there was nothing I could do with the tip. This story was later corroborated by an impeccable source who also confirmed that Donaldson turned puce and spat bile at the mention of my name.

7

WEE BARRY

Each year, weary journalists traipse to the HQ of the Crown Office in Edinburgh where they are told about major criminals being targeted with Proceeds of Crime laws. They politely nod their heads at the PR people and dutifully scribble lots of zeros in their notepads to represent the many, many millions of pounds supposedly seized. They then write down reheated soundbites – 'crime doesn't pay', 'hitting criminals in the pocket', 'bankrupting the Mr Bigs' – which duly receive blanket TV, radio and newspaper coverage.

This annual public relations exercise stems from the 1996 murder of investigative journalist Veronica Guerin, who was shot dead in Dublin at the age of 37 for telling the truth. Within a week of her death, the Irish government enacted the Proceeds of Crime Act which was eventually emulated in countries around the world, including Scotland. The purpose was to go after organised crime bosses who cheat conventional justice by seizing their illicit wealth, unless they can prove it legitimate. It was a game changer, we were told.

Sadly, this has evolved to become little more than a police and Crown PR exercise – a retrospective tax on low- to mid-level crooks and a generous new revenue stream for the legal profession. Yes, large sums have been recovered, but far too many of the most dangerous men at the pinnacle of organised crime remain entirely unruffled and their vast, laundered fortunes are as secure as Fort Knox. The Crown's biggest scalps have been scamming Shetland fishermen and a sanction-busting engineering firm – not quite Al Capone.

Russell Stirton, a north Glasgow criminal who had married into the McGovern family, was the first serious Scottish target. He had foolishly drawn attention to himself by selling the UK's cheapest fuel from his Springburn filling station. After Stirton's cut-price petrol became subject of a news story I'd written in 2003, the police went for him.

At the outset of the saga, when Stirton's £1 million rural pad was raided by detectives with the media in tow, the name of Barry Hughes came to my attention. Hughes is no ordinary street thug. The pint-sized, preening showman sometimes drives a Rolls-Royce and seeks fame more hungrily than a talentless teen YouTuber. He manipulates useful idiots in the media to shape his false image more effectively than Lenin.

He seems to have persuaded himself that he is a successful and legitimate businessman, which he is not. Hughes is not stupid so must be either too vain or too arrogant to realise that police chiefs and Crown lawyers like nothing less than cocky criminals who draw attention to themselves. In the early 2000s he was an average young boxer whose toothy grin occasionally featured on the sports pages. But his stock was rising in the underworld, where some spoke in awe of 'Wee Barry'. His risible ring nickname 'Braveheart' was adopted by his security company, a favoured business sector of gangsters. When his name cropped up in the Stirton case, I learned that the suburban Bishopbriggs home of his father, Donald

Hughes, was one of 11 other addresses visited during investigations.

Strangely, the police press office steadfastly and repeatedly denied that this was the case. I told them they were being misled by senior officers and, eventually, once I named the officers who attended the Hughes address, a high-ranking police chief backed down and, in a call to the editor of the *Sunday Mail*, admitted that my information was spot on. It was an unnecessary falsehood from the police, but why? One explanation was they may have been trying to do Hughes a turn by attempting to keep him out of the public spotlight, while at the same time allowing Stirton to believe his young friend was getting some heat. This would certainly explain Stirton's later mistrust of Hughes, which almost resulted in serious violence with one flashpoint at a favoured hangout, an upmarket Italian restaurant.

With confirmation of the Hughes address serving as a green light, we were able to put him on the news pages where he belonged. We told how Hughes, then aged 25, was at the centre of the Stirton Proceeds of Crime case and that police were examining links between the two. The story laid bare expensive properties at prestigious addresses, five-star hotel trips, flash cars worth more then the average house and public shows of wealth at charity auctions. It later emerged that Hughes once had £15,000 of cash in a Sugar Puffs cereal box to buy private hire cars for Stirton.

Following my obligatory attempt to contact Hughes prior to publication, he sought an immediate meeting with me through a middleman, a former CID officer. I was not in the habit of making my face known to criminals and declined, knowing that whatever he wanted to say could be done by phone, email or lawyer. Perhaps too, Hughes reckoned there could be some kind of deal, a trade-off, which would see us go gently on him. No deal. Undeterred by my rejection and confirming my suspicion of intended manipulation, a close associate spent the next few years passing me information about Hughes and major organised criminals. I used the information if it was valid and it checked out, but simultaneously embraced, investigated and published any tip-offs from elsewhere about Hughes. If the apparent proxy thought that drip-feeding me intelligence about other criminals would deter me from pursuing Hughes, they were mistaken. No punches were pulled.

As my refusal to meet this unspoken expectation became apparent, Hughes sought out other journalists who proved more receptive to deals. The essence of the dynamic was that Hughes would tip off the journalists with stories about himself. The journalist would then publish it. Many of these stories fuelled a false portrayal of Hughes as a pseudo-celebrity in a country where real ones are thin on the ground. As part of the sweetheart deal, the journalists airbrushed the uglier aspects of Hughes's life, creating a more palatable persona of cheeky-chappie business 'tycoon'.

Our initial exposé of Hughes was followed up with the revelation that he had been a prison visitor to Jamie 'The Iceman' Stevenson, the major drugs boss who was suspected of murdering Stirton's brother-in-law, Tony McGovern. Whispered high-security jail sit-downs with one of the country's biggest gangsters hardly fitted the image of a squeaky-clean young hotshot. Hughes was stung by The Iceman story but it did nothing to diminish his appetite for media attention and manipulation. As well as his covert channels to the news press, he sought overt coverage too, and where better than the less sceptical environs of the sports pages? He spent years telling

anyone prepared to listen that he was an upright citizen.
It was jealousy, he explained. They were all jealous of his
'success'. He told the *Daily Record* sports pages in 2006,
'People in Scotland will forgive you anything except success. What they don't know about you, they make up.' The
following year he told *The Herald* that 'here, they forgive
anything but success', and the *Daily Express* that 'people
in Scotland will forgive you anything but success, and that
attitude is increasingly frustrating'.

The most nauseating example of his self-serving prattle
was published in the sports pages of Edinburgh-based
newspaper *Scotland on Sunday* in 2008, which contained
his obligatory mantra: 'Scotland will forgive you anything
but success. That's a true saying.' It then hailed him as
'the most positive man in Glasgow' and empathised with
his press woes thus: 'It's all there in the tabloids, truth and
fiction.' The article continued:

> His theory on Glasgow is that some people want
> to believe the worst. They look at him driving
> around in his £350,000 Rolls-Royce Phantom
> Drophead and they think he can't be legit. They
> read stories linking him with imprisoned crooks
> like Jamie 'Iceman' Stevenson and they see him
> as one of them. They never look any deeper than
> surface level and it makes him sick.
>
> They ask, 'Where'd you get your money from?'
> and he tells them. But do they listen? He says if
> they stopped being consumed by jealousy and
> hate for a minute they'd be better off. Not that
> that is ever likely to happen.

Hughes then gave the paper's readers a flash of raw
conceit, expressing the view that 'Glasgow should be

honoured I still live here'. With no abatement of its breathless admiration, the article finally concluded:

> He sees it [a possible return to boxing] as his last hurrah before Braveheart goes global, before it crosses the border and travels the Atlantic, before the name Barry Hughes is up there with his ally, Frank Warren.
>
> And the begrudgers? He'll wave at them out the window of his Rolls-Royce or his Ferrari. Let them alone with their suspicion, he says. Meanwhile, he's got places to go, people to meet, mountains to climb.

The article – longer than this entire chapter – made a brief reference to Hughes being charged with carrying a knife in a nightclub but he swatted away this sticky issue by saying that 'he feels he's been wrongly accused'. Within weeks, a sheriff in Glasgow found him guilty. Presumably the sheriff did not take *Scotland on Sunday* over breakfast. Hughes tried to beat the rap by concocting what the prosecutor called an 'utterly incredible' story. A crony – who happened to be another Iceman associate – lied to the court by saying the blade belonged to him.

A year later and Hughes was convicted of punching, kicking and stamping on a man's head and body in the VIP room of another Glasgow nightclub. He was part of a mob who swarmed around the lone victim, who suffered stab and slash wounds and was struck with a metal pole. Not quite Queensberry Rules.

These two convictions may have KO'd lesser men but Hughes, like a deluded, punch-drunk pugilist, staggered back to his feet and dealt with his critics head on the only way he knew how – with his favourite soundbite. He told the *Daily Express*: 'Scotland will forgive you anything but success. That's a true saying.'

Now a convicted thug and knife-carrier with proven gangland connections, his definition of success had proved to be resilient and elastic. It would soon become even more distorted. Wee Barry was addicted to the lime-light, no matter the cost.

8

LAST ORDERS

Just audible over the babble of thirsty newspaper journal-ists came the Nokia ringtone from the inside pocket of my shiny, double-breasted suit. I pulled out the half-brick handset, extended its aerial and stepped from the smoky fug of the Copy Cat pub onto the Clydeside pavement. The caller, American-accented, introduced himself. I grabbed a pen and urgently scribbled his every word on to the small white areas of a pack of Marlboro Lights, hoping the shorthand scrawl would never be needed in court. Texan billionaire and two-time US presidential can-didate Ross Perot had called to talk about his funding of a medical research project in Scotland. Having phoned his office earlier, I had gone for a Friday-night pint, expect-ing to hear nothing. His surprise call was a lesson learned: always take the direct approach. Whether hitting a hos-tile door in a Gorbals high-rise or making a nuisance of yourself with the rich and powerful, even in today's era of digital communication and PR ubiquity, going direct remains an effective means of getting the information you need.

I moved from *The Glaswegian* to the *Sunday Mail* in 1995, when newspapers were strong, confident and still read by just about everyone, although sales were heading in one direction. Managing editor Malcolm Speed, an old-school newspaper gent and as sharp as a tack, imparted the staccato advice that if I came up with exclusive stories I would keep my job. The *Sunday Mail* – from its office in the towering *Daily Record* building at Anderston Quay – was a journalistic powerhouse read by half the population of Scotland. Editor Jim Cassidy used its massive sales as a force for good by loyally fighting for its readers, poking politicians in the ribs and sticking its nose where it was not welcome.

The Copy Cat, a smoke-filled shoebox of a pub in the shadow of the office and directly underneath the Kingston Bridge, was a hive of life despite the lack of natural light within. Finger-jabbing arguments fizzled out as quickly as they flared up between journalists standing around a podium which was a trading post for outrageous stories and filthy jokes, shared under a haze of cigarette smoke. There was nowhere to hide from cruel, razor-sharp West of Scotland wit. To refuse a drink was taken as a personal slight. Anyone attempting to duck their round was publicly called out. A payphone in the corner rang frequently – bosses hunting AWOL employees, wives on the warpath for wayward husbands. The calls often resulted in rosy-cheeked subs scurrying from their stools, blinking into the daylight and weaving back to their desks or homes.

Junkie shoplifters would discreetly open Berghaus jackets to magically reveal pilfered wares – dayglo orange blocks of cheese, prescription glasses from opticians' displays, chilled bottles of champagne.

Anyone drunk enough to give backchat to the Copy Cat's terrifyingly formidable barmaid, Anna Houston, would feel the sting of her leather strap on their backside, administered to jeers from greasy-haired men in crumpled raincoats. Her son Billy took cheques from trusted

regulars in exchange for cash from the till as there was no
ATM in this dark corner of the city. No one ever passed a
rubber cheque. At closing time, those heading to a party
could stock up with a case of beer or a bottle of spirits –
the deal being that the free carryout must be replaced the
next day. And it wasn't just a place for old men – the misty-
eyed 'When I . . .' tribe who could talk incessantly about
the good old days. Thriving newspapers drew a healthy
intake of young staff.

Outside the pub was an endless procession of Croft private hire cars. Most journalists had a pocketful of yellow
chits which gave free rides, paid by the company. One
journalist found himself dispatched to Dornoch to cover
Madonna's wedding after a colleague had been ordered
home for getting into a scrape in a local pub. Without a
driving licence and with only a clinking carrier bag in the
footwell to keep him occupied, the substitute was taken
210 miles in a Croft car. The taxi chits were abused on an
industrial scale and the bean counters eventually put paid
to them. Widespread expenses abuses would also be cur-
tailed. Three football hacks once submitted claims that
they had each lunched with Partick Thistle manager John
Lambie. The only puzzle was how they had all done so on
the same day and in different places.

The howff's other clientele resided in the adjacent
homeless hostel. It was not always easy to tell the two groups
apart. Long-term hostel resident Old Howard beamed a
toothless grin while collecting empties in exchange for
a drink. When he passed away, a blue tin of Tennent's
Super Lager was placed respectfully atop his coffin.

Newspapers were on a cusp. Ever-downward sales
would eventually neuter strong editors like Cassidy, who
were often replaced by plastic company men, subordin-
ated to accountants. Cassidy once told a gormless but

ambitious executive from the West Midlands: 'I thought that Benny from *Crossroads* was the stupidest person from Birmingham – until I met you.' Benny ended up running the company. Future editors would learn their place. Journalists became expected, then required, to stay at their desks rather than disappear in pursuit of a story.

On the brink of the millennium, the landmark red *Daily Record* monolith was reduced to rubble with its replacement seemingly inspired by a soulless car showroom. The old building's printing press, its loud beating heart, was transplanted to a grey motorway business park.

The Copy Cat fought to stay alive after the new building opened but, year after year, staff numbers were decimated. When the hostel closed, the pub clung to life but it was just a question of time. A tipping point came when greater numbers of youthful journalists went for a lunchtime jog than a pint – to the open-mouthed disgust of the diminishing old guard.

Society, as well as newspapers, was changing. In the decade after Ross Perot called me in 1998, the lunchtime pint went from being nearly compulsory to an occasional exercise in nostalgia and then highly unusual – a suspicion of possible alcoholism. Now it's a sackable offence.

After joining Scotland's biggest-selling paper at the age of 22, I regaled friends who worked in boring, normal jobs about the crazy merry-go-round. I joked that the *Sunday Mail* was a pub that produced a newspaper. I was still little more than a kid with a lot to learn, but there was no better place to do so. I had a plastic bag in the boot of my car, ever expanding with little blue Nicolson maps of towns and villages in every corner of Scotland.

One day the boss sent me into Ravenscraig, the massive former steelworks in Motherwell which had closed four years earlier in 1992. A 16-year-old boy had fallen to his death while scavenging for copper. We breached security to join teams of grimy-faced men harvesting scrap from the dirty and dangerous site, dotted with fires, which resembled a scene from the post-apocalyptic movie *Mad Max*. We investigated claims that security guards were taking payments from scavengers to drive their heavy hauls of metal off the site. The job resulted in me having to give evidence to a fatal accident enquiry into the boy's death. When asked to name the rogue guards, I could only squirm while offering the hushed court their nicknames – 'Shagger 1' and 'Shagger 2' – as this was how they were referred to by the scavengers.

One early investigation centred on a flamboyant developer flogging plots of land to build dream homes. The plots were worthless and the businessman was a bankrupt thug with convictions for violence and extortion. He thought it was a good idea to name one of his companies Semper Ebrius Ltd (Latin for 'always drunk').

A contact told me about a 15-year-old criminal, a baby-faced 'one-boy crime wave' in Glasgow's deprived Castlemilk housing estate. He had shot his social worker, committed armed robbery, dealt drugs, burgled and set fire to houses, but the authorities seemed powerless to rein him in. The feral boy's home was unlike any I have ever been in – bare, filthy and cold. His family were utterly dysfunctional and the poverty oppressive. The newspaper starkly warned that worse was to come. A year later he was jailed for murder, having stamped and kicked an innocent man to death in the street for no apparent reason.

The *Sunday Mail* was big on unmasking the kind of 'businessmen' who make money by ripping off decent, hard-working people. A photographer captured me rummaging in a giant industrial wheelie bin, trying to find an address for a crook who had stiffed our readers for their savings. One of my first such targets was Andrew Best, who scammed fortunes while simultaneously using the local press to portray himself as a business titan bringing hundreds of jobs to Cumbernauld. When I confronted him, he brazenly denied that the Andrew Best with a history of seven failed companies he was – despite the same name, date of birth and confirmation of his ID by numerous victims. A decade later, Best graduated from dodgy firms flogging vacuum cleaners and exterior house painting to drug-dealing, which did not end well. He finally ripped off the wrong people. Gangster David Hughes lured Best to meet him at a garden centre where he stabbed him 16 times. With his dying breath, Best named Hughes to police and the killer was caught.

A particularly odd job was being dispatched to a small Fife village to visit what appeared to be a regular shop offering clothing alterations and repairs. Shoppers who explained what they were *really* looking for were ushered through a curtain into a secret back shop – a boutique for cross-dressing men with Polaroids of happy customers adorning one wall. I was joined by an older female photographer posing as my understanding girlfriend. She stifled giggles as I tottered dangerously out of the changing cubicle clad in a figure-hugging gold lamé mini-skirt and size 11 patent leather slingbacks with six-inch heels. My unusual expenses claim for these purchases was approved. My only defence is that these were less enlightened times than today.

Faxes were used daily but the *Sunday Mail* also had a thing called the internet. A veteran reporter, a self-styled Bill Gates, jealously guarded the only computer with online access. A few months later, his Russian bride arrived in Scotland.

As grateful as I am to have caught the dying days of press hedonism and largesse, I am glad that the music stopped when it did. Far too many of the earlier generations of journalists could not get off the merry-go-round, and the music never stopped for them. They lived fast, drunk and chaotically. Their marriages were destroyed, their children neglected. After being forced out the door, bitter and broken, it was only a short shuffle to an early grave.

The month after the Perot call, I joined the *News of the World*. The move was necessary for me to secure a mortgage as the *News of the World* offered a staff job instead of temporary contracts. The short hop across the river to Kinning Park felt like leaving a funfair for a high-security prison. The building was a red-brick, windowless Lubyanka where sightings of rats were not uncommon. Glasgow staff were flown to London to attend the Christmas party. The aloof London reporters – all stripy shirts and red braces – were like braying stockbrokers.

One colleague bragged about having sex with prostitutes but was less candid about his rumoured financial stake in their business. His main contact, the biggest player in Glasgow's vice scene, benefited from *News of the World* protection. This contact was connected to major drug-dealer Tam 'The Licensee' McGraw and, like him, was suspected of being a police informant. As well as trading in flesh, the vice king produced and sold porn videos under the counter from his chain of shops. Other newspapers were morally outraged over material which is now mainstream. More deserving of their ire was the criminal's alleged blackmailing of people who were lured to take part in wife-swapping events through the pages of his swingers' publication. These parties were stage-managed with prostitutes playing the roles of partners or wives. Participants, all respectable people, were warned to pay up or else – the 'or else' being that their sexual antics would end up in the *News of the World*.

As I sat in the office late one Saturday night, the early edition of the *Sunday Mail* landed. My rogue colleague immediately turned to an exposé of the vice empire of his contact and proceeded to phone him. He duly provided a detailed description of the article and then, to my astonishment, told his contact that he knew which town the *Sunday Mail* journalist lived in and that he would find out his address. I was speechless. A colleague had brazenly provided personal information about a fellow journalist to a gangster, simply because he had written an entirely truthful story about the gangster's illegal activities. I had no choice but to alert my former colleague, who was grateful and angry in equal measure. He phoned the *News of the World* man to tell him to back off, which was met with protestations of feigned innocence.

Drugs buys were a staple exercise at the *News of the World*. Reporters ditched their shirt and tie, hooked up with a junkie and hit a door where drugs were sold. One such job saw me securing heroin and amphetamines from a family who had won a competition run by Coca-Cola to have their garden transformed into a dazzling Christmas light display. It produced the headline 'COKE PAYS FOR LIGHTING . . . HEROIN AND SPEED FOOT REST OF THE BILLS'. Such dealers were deserving of exposure but they were really just desperate minions being used to peddle tenner-bags from their homes by the people who supplied them – the people who really needed press attention.

I was relieved when the *Sunday Mail* asked me to return. I had lasted eight months at the *News of the World*. That it was later exposed as a den of 'dark arts', criminality and sleaze came as no surprise to me.

9

DOMESTIC *OMERTÀ*

Bug-eyed and with his mouth twisted in hate, Frankie Donaldson feels the warm glow of familiar pleasure as his fist slams hard into human flesh. The snarling gangster looms over his cowed victim, whose garbled pleas for mercy are futile. If anything, they only sharpen his visceral lust for violence. His hand shoots out and snatches a clump of hair, twisting and yanking it so tightly in his grip that dark red soaks the roots. The victim switches to survival mode, becoming a limp rag doll while praying for it to end.

The petrified victim is dragged outside by the hair across a gravel driveway and bundled into a car. If anyone hears the screams for help, they know better than to get involved. Donaldson's finale to this short and brutal eruption is to repeatedly slam his victim's face into the steering wheel, leaving it a bruised and bloody pulp. With a triumphant smirk, he savours the soaring high of pure gratification.

The victim was not some underworld rival but Jane Clarke, his long-term partner and the mother of his son. Confident, well educated and outgoing from a loving family, she is a strong and independent businesswoman with a background in social work who built a successful chain of children's nurseries. She still does not understand how she became a serial victim of extreme domestic violence at the hands of the man she loved. What's even harder to understand is how it took her more than 20 years to escape.

Jane met Donaldson in her mid twenties. He was a decade older, a swaggering wise guy rolling in cash and feared by many. Other gangsters shrank at the mention of his name, which opened every door in the city. Being Frankie's girl was a thrill. No one messes with Frankie Donaldson.

Like many domestic abusers, it was all about control. He burned with jealousy whenever she spoke to another man. His solution was a chaperone. When Jane left the house she was shadowed by a hulking nightclub bouncer, paid in cash by Donaldson to scare off men from sniffing about. It wasn't long before the violence started. Over the course of their 22-year relationship, she lost count of the number of assaults but estimates that it was well over 100. It soon became 'normal', almost routine, like putting out the bin or brushing your teeth. He used his fists and feet but also reached for weapons – bottles, car keys, dumb-bells, mobile phones, a TV remote control. She will always have an indention from where he brought a dumbbell crashing down on her skull. A car key taken to her face, which required six stitches, also caused scarring for life. The rules of engagement were unspoken but explicit. Following an assault, she was prohibited from seeking any medical treatment for her injuries – unless they were too serious to ignore. She was also banned from ever discussing any attack with him or anyone else – a weird domestic *omertà*, as if they never happened.

Having stepped out of the shower in a rage, Donaldson once tightened a towel around her neck and watched her slowly turn purple. Frantic for air, Jane thought the last thing she would ever see would be his face, a venomous and spitting gargoyle of hate. He eventually eased the pressure and she filled her lungs with air, blinking back tears. She was aware of the rules – no doctors and no discussion.

Jane's sister Liz was another victim. She had the guts to stand up to Donaldson. This he could not tolerate and he responded the only way he knew. On one occasion, Donaldson seized Liz by the throat and pinned her against the window of her mother's second-floor flat while threatening to throw her to the pavement below.

It was in 2013 on the island of Majorca, after the sun had set on a beautiful July day, that Donaldson committed his final act of violence against Jane. He was in a vile mood and stormed out of a restaurant in Palma where he and Jane were dining with their son and two other young children. When she and the kids arrived back at the house, he was brooding and waiting. The violence was instant and sustained. Unusually, he did not observe his traditional nicety of waiting until they were alone. The terrified children witnessed all hell break loose. Fighting for her life and screaming for help, Jane was silenced with a bottle smashed over her head which knocked her out cold. The children thought she was dead. Her screams had been heard and the police arrived. The sickened Spanish officers dispensed some instant justice against Donaldson of the type rarely applied any more by British police.

Paramedics urged Jane to go to hospital but she declined as she could not abandon the children to the Spanish authorities. They packed their suitcases and went straight to Palma airport, where they were told it was nine hours until the first plane back to Scotland. During the long wait, under the bright departure-lounge lights, thousands of travellers gawped at the black, blue and bloody-faced woman with three tired and confused kids. It was one of the only occasions where she took a photo of Donaldson's handiwork. She later discovered that she should not have flown as the bottle blow had caused bleeding on the brain. As horrific as the Majorca attack was, it was not the worst that she had suffered, although it would make the all-time top ten.

Back in Scotland, they were met by Liz, who issued a tough-love ultimatum. She told Jane that if she returned to Donaldson, then she would seek custody of their son. Returning would be to put her own life, as well as the boy's life, at serious risk from a man who was clearly out of control and potentially capable of anything. Jane knew that her sister was right. There could be no away back – not this time. Before Donaldson returned from Majorca, she removed their belongings from the family home in the affluent Glasgow suburb of Bearsden and found a new place to live, a refuge from decades of domestic oppression.

But if she thought that Donaldson, the ultimate control freak, would simply shrug his shoulders, put it down to experience and leave it at that, she was mistaken. What followed was a campaign in which guilt and guile, terror and threats were deployed in an attempt to break her down, force her into submission and crawl back to him.

Friends, well-meaning but oblivious to the truth, turned up at her door pleading, 'Come on, Jane, you know Frankie loves you. Think of everything he's done for you.' No one expected contrition but Donaldson seemed to believe that he was really a good guy and that it was just a fuss over nothing. Some made excuses, saying that whisky and cocaine were responsible for Donaldson's explosions of violence, but that was nonsense. Often he was stone-cold sober.

This tone of approach lasted until October. That's
when Donaldson realised she was not coming back. He
turned to tactics of terror. Anonymous rats from the
underworld popped up mouthing threats before slipping
away. Jane's every move was tracked, confirmed by text
messages which revealed where she had been morning,
noon and night. She existed on a knife-edge, in a state
of paranoia and anxious anticipation that something very
bad could happen at any moment.

One text message said that William 'Basil' Burns was
going to shoot a child witness – the same Burns who
later turned up at my door with a bottle of acid. Another
text warned Jane that a woman had been paid to throw
acid in her face while she was doing the school run. The
threat was explicit, detailed and chilling. Another threat
was made to shoot a child relative who is autistic. None
of this could be readily dismissed. These people were
deadly serious. The texts all came from throwaway pay-
as-you-go mobiles, bought with cash, which meant they
were untraceable. She, her friends, family and nursery
colleagues were in the firing line of the unrelenting
campaign of intimidation. They were bombarded for
five months.

During this time, Jane and her business were also targeted by state agencies – HMRC, the Care Commission,
Police Scotland. Vexatious allegations were made against
her – tax evasion, money-laundering, mortgage fraud,
nursery regulation breaches – all of which had to be investigated, even once she had explained to the civil servants
that they were being used as puppets by a domestic abuser
to attack and break her. The pressure was immense, with
every intrusive challenge from faceless officialdom taking
great effort, time and money to put right. These government agencies became dupes – tools in Donaldson's

systematic campaign of abuse. But, they explained, they were obliged to investigate.

Her new home soon felt more like a trap than a refuge. The shooting threats instilled a fear of putting on living-room lights during darkness, as she would become an easy target. So she commando-crawled around the unlit house on her belly to stay below window-level and used the beam of her phone to illuminate her way between rooms.

Donaldson made noises about how she had been seen at Glasgow airport getting on a flight to Dubai when she was actually in Glasgow. Associates were told that she had cruelly dumped poor Frankie for a mysterious millionaire. Later she was accused of having an affair with a senior police officer. Eventually, she was supposed to be involved with me. All of these stories were fiction and either the product of Donaldson's jealous imagination or perhaps an attempt at saving face.

By early December 2013 her resolve began to crack and she made a tentative approach to a specialised police unit whose officers deal with domestic abuse crime. Still too scared to give a statement, she just wanted to see what her options were. Throughout the subsequent weeks, the pressure increased. Not only did she have a virtual target on her back 24/7, she felt responsible for others being put in jeopardy, including innocent children, relatives, friends and colleagues.

The turning point came on the evening of Boxing Day 2013, when Liz's husband phoned Jane in a panic. Donaldson had come to his door and said that a gunman was already on the way to shoot Jane that night at her home in the city's west end. Donaldson also allegedly threatened that Liz would be getting shot as well. Jane believed his threats to be credible so called 999. The police arrived quickly and escorted her from her home.

From there, they drove to a theatre in the city where Jane's son was with his aunt Liz and another child watching a pantomime. The police insisted they had to leave the panto immediately for their own safety.

During five months of torture, Jane's attempts at reason had not worked and she knew that to back down now and surrender would be impossible. Trusting the police – and their all-powerful masters at the Crown Office – was all that was available to her, but it felt like a Hobson's choice. Had Donaldson accepted the relationship was over after Majorca, then Jane would not have been driven into the arms of the police. Maybe he later realised that by forcing her hand, he had brought the police upon himself.

The two sisters were taken to different police stations where they provided detailed statements about every aspect of Donaldson's 22-year reign of terror. The following night, 27 December, the police tracked him down and made the arrest. After being locked up for the weekend, he was taken to the city's Sheriff Court on Monday, 30 December. Led upstairs in handcuffs, he stood in the dock facing a single charge of assault to injury but there was more, much more, to come. To his outrage, Donaldson was remanded in custody for seven days. He welcomed in 2014 behind bars.

Bail was granted at his next court appearance on 7 January. In the meantime, the domestic abuse unit's officers had been busy building a bigger case against him. Of the scores of incidents revealed by Jane and Liz, the police prioritised those where other witnesses could provide the corroboration required to secure a conviction. They charged Donaldson with another seven assaults, two breaches of the peace and one of making threats, resulting in another court appearance on 13 January. This time, his lawyers managed to secure bail.

Jane was still struggling to deal with the feelings of guilt and angst for 'grassing', an ethos ingrained in too many a Glaswegian mind. It was during this time that she finally broke. She was in a mess – unable to effectively communicate, rationalise or fully function. Her entire body would shake uncontrollably. Partly this came from the absolute relief and release of taking such a momentous step after so many years of subjugation. Friends and family urged her to seek help and she was diagnosed with post-traumatic stress disorder. Her counsellor said that some military cases of PTSD he had treated were not as acute as hers.

The police had got themselves a very big catch indeed. Donaldson ticked two big boxes in terms of the priorities of political-led policing – domestic violence and organised crime. More charges were to follow.

Jane had taken the first step on an extremely dangerous path. She reluctantly put her faith in the police, the Crown Office and the judiciary, and could only hope that they would honour their part of the deal by delivering justice and doing so swiftly and fairly.

One problem – no one messes with Frankie Donaldson.

10

AFFAIR PRICE

While Frankie Donaldson brought the police upon himself by inflicting violence on his partner, the major woes of Barry Hughes were caused by cheating on his.

Hughes was under police surveillance when he left his wife and children at home for what he assumed would be a secret tryst in London with a former Miss Scotland. By chance, the *Sunday Mail* newspaper already had a team there kicking its heels on another story when a tip came through from a freelance with impeccable police contacts: 'Wee Barry Hughes is up to naughties at The Berkeley Hotel with ex-Miss Scotland Michelle Watson.'

From a discreet vantage point, a photographer captured the beaming lovers emerging hand-in-hand from the five-star hotel in Knightsbridge. They returned to their opulent suite after a romantic lunch spent gazing into each other's eyes and hammering his credit card in high-end boutiques.

Betrayed Jackie, his wife of three years, was devastated, telling the newspaper, 'I had no idea. He told me he was away on business. I just feel humiliated.'

Watson, also aghast, said, 'I was unaware that Barry had got back together with his wife because, as far as I was concerned, he was legally separated.'

When his affair became public, Hughes turned to his friends in the press in order to put a positive spin on the news coverage. This may have made him feel slightly better but, ultimately, he could do nothing to shape what was unfolding at home.

Jackie's shock, pain and humiliation hardened into scorn. While the £750-a-night hotel suite and Miss Scotland's shopping spree at Harvey Nichols and Harrods was expensive, the real cost, to be paid years down the line, would be much higher. Jackie kicked him out and called a divorce lawyer who filed court documents seeking a slice of his fortune. Crucially, they contained the assertion that Jackie was 'financially dependent' on her husband and that she had not done a single day's paid work in the seven years since 2000.

She later forgave the infidelity – the gift of a new Bentley helping soothe the pain – and the divorce lawyers were muzzled. But, unbeknown to them both at the time, the damage was done. Jackie's financial statements would come back to bite them, almost sending them both to prison.

The documents were a time bomb which lay in a file for three years until 2010, when police seized them during a raid on the family's 11-bedroom home in a gated enclave in Kilmacolm, Renfrewshire. The raid became a circus. One enterprising police officer got a ticking off but deserved a commendation – for erecting a sign which stated: 'Police: tackling serious and organised crime.' Even worse than that were the police's toilet habits. Indignant Hughes planted a story in *The Scottish Sun* in which a 'pal' complained about them using all his toilet paper, not flushing and leaving the house 'smelling'.

Hughes spent that night in a police cell (his view of the toilet facilities is unknown) and the following day appeared in court facing three mortgage fraud charges relating to different properties and two of obtaining money unlawfully. After returning from a holiday in Spain, Jackie then stood in a court dock charged with three counts of deception, including money laundering and mortgage fraud.

Many people may have a vague notion about the courts and justice system being creaky and inefficient. We've all heard anecdotes about chaotic jury service and read the news diet of bungled prosecutions resulting in nasty criminals getting off the hook. But many people would be surprised at how venal and inept it really is. The first thing to understand is that the criminal justice system appears to have been created by lawyers for lawyers. Justice seems to be a mere afterthought. So, when criminals with deep pockets want to play games, there is no stopping them. One of the favourite tactics of the wealthy and well-connected is to 'churn' a case, which is to come up with spurious excuses to cause as many delays as possible. Open-and-shut prosecutions, which should take months, disappear into a black hole for years. The longer a case remains in limbo, the greater the chance that witnesses can be nobbled, lose heart, forget their evidence or die. This cynical exercise in attrition causes cases to collapse due to a time bar or weary prosecutors making a mistake or simply giving up. At the very least, the churn culture, orchestrated by greedy defence lawyers, gives criminals free rein to get on with their real business without any distractions.

Hughes first appeared in court in July 2010 but was not convicted until February 2014. For 1,309 days he tied the process up in knots. Hughes initially hired lawyer Paul McBride QC, a razor-sharp legal Mr Fixit with his finger in many pies. McBride's USP was that he could pull strings with his high-level contacts in the Crown

Office. If the price was right, he could get charges to disappear or, where that was impossible, secure favourable plea deals. Unfortunately for Hughes, McBride died in Pakistan in 2012 while on a mission to negotiate the return of an alleged £50-million fugitive fraudster. It has never been explained whether McBride was there with the authority, official or unofficial, of his friends at the Crown.

When Hughes was finally convicted in 2014, he and Jackie stood together in the dock. Even without McBride, the defence lawyers managed to secure a deal. The motivation of the Crown was to get a result. Given that four years had elapsed, they seemed willing to do so at just about any price. The terms of the deal were that Hughes – possibly through pragmatism rather than spousal chivalry – plead guilty to some charges while all those against pregnant Jackie were dropped. Hughes had lied to get a £430,000 mortgage by claiming his wife earned £160,000 from an interior design business. The £129,000 profit from selling that first house became laundered money, acquired through the initial fraud. Hughes then told another lender the same lie in order to get an £858,000 mortgage. The big lies about Jackie's bogus earnings were nailed thanks to the forgotten divorce document – in which she truthfully stated she had earned nothing since 2000. Hughes's cheating had come at a heavy price.

Sheriff Alan Mackenzie then jailed him for 43 months, saying, 'The fact remains that the deception you engaged in was not only audacious, involving extravagant claims to secure very substantial loans, but was also repeated.' Hughes appealed successfully against the jail sentence and a *Scottish Sun* photographer was arranged to capture him strutting cockily from HMP Barlinnie after a few weeks, his sentence reduced to a £45,000 fine.

When Jackie gave birth shortly afterwards, Hughes clicked his fingers and another photographer was in place for the family leaving hospital with their new arrival. The paper carried a photo of Hughes stepping into a £235,0000 Rolls-Royce. Not a single word accompanying the photos referred to his criminality.

Hughes then let it be known to the same paper that he casually paid his £45,000 fine with a debit card, as if it were a mere speeding ticket. All of this was PR with the intent to gloat, and it left a foul taste in the mouths of anyone with knowledge of what Hughes really is – a violent, knife-carrying, money-laundering fraudster with major gangland connections.

A few months prior to these pro-Hughes stories, I had joined *The Scottish Sun* as Investigations Editor. My job was to go after major organised crime figures along with corrupt politicians, bent lawyers, dodgy judges and crooked cops. The newspaper's relationship with Hughes did not sit comfortably with me. One wonders what Sheriff Mackenzie and the dozens of hard-working police officers and Crown lawyers who brought Hughes to justice thought about it.

Then one day I got tip from a contact telling me to look at Jackie's Twitter account. The Hughes family had taken an expensive holiday to Dubai. Jackie – perhaps believing Barry's oft-repeated claim of being 'legit' – had plastered their holiday snaps online. They flew business class on Emirates, stayed in a £1,600-a-night suite at the seven-star Burj Al Arab hotel and had been collected from the airport in a chauffeur-driven Rolls-Royce. One snap showed them chatting to their personal butler. The estimated cost of the lavish trip was equivalent to around double the annual salary of an average worker.

I unearthed new information about how much taxpayers' money had been paid to the couple's lawyers during the four-year fraud saga. The Scottish Legal Aid Board admitted that they had handed over £95,000 to Jackie's legal team and £81,000 to Hughes'. Furthermore, he was *still* raking in legal aid to contest an ongoing Proceeds of Crime case. Solicitors love to complain about hardship whenever legal aid budgets fall under political scrutiny – their most emotional argument being that cuts deny justice to the poor. Such claims are nonsense. The £176,000 paid to Hughes and Jackie was obscene. How could the police and Crown present evidence that he is a multimillionaire criminal while, simultaneously, another branch of the state deems him to be so hard up that taxpayers should foot his monstrous legal bills?

I spoke to the Labour MSP Graeme Pearson, who was well known to Hughes and his sort from years spent as a detective then police chief. Pearson nailed it with his comment: 'It's bizarre in these circumstances that he continues to receive legal aid at great cost to the taxpayer. How can someone like this receive legal aid when many ordinary, hard-working people are unable to? It defies logic.' Scottish Conservative justice spokeswoman Margaret Mitchell agreed, saying, 'It is becoming increasingly common for criminals who've made fortunes from illicit acts to be able to get off by paying almost nothing. This undermines the whole justice system, making it a laughing stock among the criminal community.'

The brutal and critical report, published in *The Scottish Sun* on 26 October 2014, exposing the gross misuse of public money, was not the kind of fawning coverage that he was used to. He was not happy with me, I was told. I didn't care, I replied.

Two months later, as his Dubai suntan was fading, Hughes declared himself bankrupt with personal debts of around £10 million. Most of this money was owed to the tax man, and the decision by Hughes to go bust, hand-picking his own trustee, appears to have been a pre-emptive move in the Proceeds of Crime case being waged against him.

A few weeks afterwards, I had an odd encounter involving Hughes. As I stood in a city-centre Sainsbury's queue with a lunchtime sandwich, Hughes strode in the door and stopped just level with where I was standing. My fist clenched by side, my nostrils invaded by his pungent aftershave, I tensed in anticipation of having to whack him with my baguette. He clocked me and, without speaking a word, turned and left. Given the type of people I had investigated, I was careful never to have my photo online. I suspected the Hughes associate who had spent years passing me information had clocked me going into Sainsbury's. Perhaps he wanted to know what I looked like up close. I was concerned enough to mention it to a handful of trusted friends and colleagues. If he started taking it personally, I could have a problem.

At the beginning of 2015 I produced a six-day series about organised crime in Scotland. One day was devoted to female criminals and their typical roles, which often involve mortgages, company directorships and administrative issues. Under the headline 'GIRL POWER', we explained how the Crown was using a novel tactic of jointly putting gangsters and their wives or girlfriends in the dock. This gave the prosecutors leverage which often resulted in the men striking a plea deal in exchange for the mother of their children being spared prison. One example cited was the case of Barry and Jackie Hughes. He was incandescent with rage and, at 8.30 a.m., phoned the mobile of my boss, Gordon Smart, who was then editor of *The Scottish Sun*.

Smart told me that the call from Hughes had been '45 minutes of fury'. I was surprised; most editors would have nothing to do with a gangland thug such as Hughes, let alone give them 45 minutes of their time. It was only much later that I discovered Hughes had said plenty more about me during the call.

11

MAÑANA, MAÑANA

For the first time in his life, Frankie Donaldson had lost control. For the first time in his life, someone had stood up to him. After 22 years of silent subservience, Jane Clarke was free, vocal and defiant. She was going to need all the strength she could possibly muster.

An anonymous call came through on my mobile: 'Donuts got lifted for battering his missus. He's been doing it for years. He hates you anyway, so do a story to really annoy him.' Donaldson's dislike of me originally stemmed from the 2001 story about the foiled plot to 'put a hole in Donuts' and, over the intervening 13 years, I had written a few others which helped drive his ludicrous legal outing to stop the press from using his nickname.

A year before learning about his domestic violence arrest, a journalist colleague had imparted fresh intelligence. He rhymed off a series of stories that particularly irked Donaldson, but I was perplexed because other reporters had written some of those on the offending list. The colleague went on to confirm the story about my car being torched – rather, someone else's car because mine had not. While not hugely taken with the caller's enthusiasm for me to pursue Donaldson just to stoke his illogical hatred towards me, I could not ignore the tip. I asked the Crown Office for details of the arrest but received a typically terse response. With no meaningful details, the story was parked.

A breakthrough came six months later with an imminent court appearance for Donaldson. Having learned that he faced 11 charges – including six of assaulting Jane and one of threatening to shoot her and her family in the head – a story was written.

Contempt laws exist to protect people charged with crimes from having prejudicial material published prior to their trial. It is deemed fair that a jury considering guilt or innocence should not know if the accused is already, for example, a convicted axe killer. But a law designed to ensure fair trials also inadvertently benefits major criminals by censoring their convictions or gangland associations. It legitimises by omission. Media lawyers love pontificating about the nuances of contempt, but it often seems to be just a guessing game as the Crown operates a pick'n'mix policy of pursuing cases at random, blithely overlooking blatant breaches when it suits them. A lawyer's interpretation, therefore, resulted in our story about Donaldson's domestic violence arrest being sanitised. No reference could be made to his gangland links. Even his nickname was prohibited – lest it somehow taint jurors' minds in some way. Instead, we had to falsely call him a 'tycoon' and 'millionaire businessman', jarring misuses of language. Barry Hughes benefited from contempt laws in exactly the same way. While his fraud and money-laundering case churned through court for 1,309 days, the press could not refer to his convictions or gangland cronies – again, legitimacy by omission.

In the digital era, it is impossible to scour the internet and remove all traces of potentially prejudicial material and, given that jurors are under strict orders to consider only evidence led in court, the time to bin or radically reform contempt laws is long overdue.

I had been picking up more chatter about Donaldson's negative view of me. A washed-up actor often seen weaving between west-end bars had been tasked with finding out information about me through a mutual associate. I phoned him to question him and warn him off. He admitted knowing Donaldson, but his protestations of innocence were unconvincing. When he then tried to incorrectly blame me for publication of a story about his own domestic violence, I knew he was lying. This recorded conversation was passed to the police following the acid attack.

Donaldson was becoming increasingly close to Barry Hughes, which was curious because, a decade earlier, there had been a brief clash when Donaldson went after a Hughes associate with no comeback. Furthermore, Donaldson grew up with Hughes' dad Donald in Calton, at the eastern edge of Glasgow city centre. Contemporaries tell how Donaldson made Hughes Sr's life miserable with bullying and violence. As well as a shared animus towards me, Donaldson and Hughes were both active in football-related business and courted big names in the sport. Huge sums of money were involved. The more I heard, the more concerned I became. I regarded both Donaldson and Hughes as highly dangerous – not least due to their thin skins. The alarm bells caused me to seek advice from ex-police chief turned Labour MSP Graeme Pearson, who knew both of them well. As a young detective, Pearson was responsible for arresting Donaldson decades earlier over resetting, or handling, stolen fur coats near the Barras market. Pearson told me, 'If Donaldson's got you on his mind, take care. He is one who would deliver. I would never usually say that to anyone. The Barry Hughes connection is significant – he will have wound up Donaldson. Don't get paranoid about it but take it seriously.'

When my story about Donaldson's 11 charges was published in November 2014, I was not long into a new personal relationship and oblivious to the freakish coincidence that my partner lived in close proximity to Jane Clarke. Since fleeing from Majorca the previous summer, Jane had sustained an onslaught of charm and menace designed to make her back down. Just like Hughes, Donaldson had plenty of money to throw at lawyers. He would stop at nothing to ensure the right result. Also like Hughes, churning was a key weapon.

The scandal of churn had been going on for decades despite the efforts at reform by senior judges and prosecutors. In 2002, the judge Lord Bonomy was tasked with reviewing the 'shambles' of courts. He identified churning as the greatest problem, with one third of cases adjourned at least once. He said, 'This change has greatly increased the distress and disruption caused to victims, relatives of victims, witnesses and jurors and may undermine public confidence in the criminal justice system. The public, quite rightly, expect that, in a modern, sophisticated legal system, it should be possible to organise business to reduce the level of distress and inconvenience.'

In 2003, Lord Advocate Colin Boyd – now a judge – said that lawyers should be censured for unnecessary delays 'if it's done purely with the intention of trying to find some loophole or to try and trip the prosecution up'.

Another judge, Lord Hamilton in 2011, gave this withering take on 'corrosive' churn: 'I find it unacceptable that cases do not proceed on the day allotted to them – unless there are exceptional and wholly justified reasons for adjournment. Those who appear ill prepared to proceed or who have been unable to ensure the attendance

of witnesses should expect close questioning from the
bench. Churn is a waste of taxpayers' money and is
inimical to the proper administration of justice.' Audit
Scotland – the government agency which examines how
taxpayers' money is spent – produced a 2015 report which
found the cost of churn in sheriff courts to be around
£10 million or £27,400 every day.

It is female victims of sexual violence and domestic
attacks who suffer most from churning, which is at odds
with the oft-proclaimed political and police intent to deal
quickly and effectively with men who harm women. In a
submission to the Scottish Parliament justice committee,
Scottish Women's Aid charity stated, 'Churn and delay is
a particular issue in relation to cases involving domestic
abuse.' Jan Macleod, of Women's Support Project charity,
told MSPs on the committee, 'Delays are very distressing
not just for the victim but also for their partner or family.
You have to get really psyched up for going to court so it
can be very hard if the case is adjourned again and again.'
The Scottish government's own guidelines attest to the
swift prosecution of such cases being vital. They state that
'fast-tracked cases have a lower incidence of victim retrac-
tion and therefore lower incidences of case attrition'.

Have these strongly worded interventions from judges,
the significant cost to the public purse and, most impor-
tantly, the plea of victims made the slightest difference to
the culture of churn? Quite clearly not. And, for as long
as the vested financial interests of the legal profession
trump the public interest, don't expect things to change,
no matter how much noise emanates from the bench or
campaigners.

The Donaldson and Hughes cases could serve as case
studies in churn. To echo the sentiment of the judges,
it trashes justice and the public's faith in it. Having first

appeared at court in December 2013, Donaldson ordered his lawyers to use every stalling tactic at their disposal. As a reporter, I stopped counting the number of times the Crown stated that the case would go ahead only for it to be kicked into the long grass. Days became weeks, weeks months and months years. 'Mañana, Mañana' should be carved into the stonework above the Crown's HQ in Chambers Street, Edinburgh.

Donaldson came up with another ruse – to use the civil justice system against his victim. He paid lawyers to sue Jane for £1 million, claiming that he had been a source of funding and business expertise to build her chain of children's nurseries. The claim was untrue but it could not simply be ignored. So, as the criminal case inched painfully through court, Jane had to invest a huge amount of time and pay good money to lawyers in order to fight the spurious civil case that she had become 'unjustly enriched' thanks to him. Just as the state agencies HMRC and Care Commission had been used as tools in the campaign of control against her, now the civil courts opened up as another front in the domestic abuse.

Donaldson's lawyers produced a list of witnesses for his claim. One name on it was Jane's mother, who had been dead for many years. During one hearing, a lawyer sniggered about calling upon 'the dead witness'. This legal action was an act of self-harm because it shone an unwelcome spotlight on Donaldson's own jealously guarded and intriguing financial affairs, opening them to public scrutiny and the eyes of state agencies.

Jane's lawyers had no choice but to respond with a counter-claim which laid bare details of how she provided money to buy a £500,000 apartment in Dubai and a £125,000 flat on the island of Cape Verde, both in Donaldson's name. Also in his name were a Majorcan bank account with a £300,000 balance and other accounts in Luxembourg and Cape Verde.

When I learned abut the civil case, I wrote an exclusive story which presumably only fuelled Donaldson's anger towards me. Due to antiquated contempt law, we could only refer to him as a 'businessman'. Twitchy lawyers were also adamant that we could not mention the parallel criminal case, even though it would not be in front of a jury any time soon, if at all. The civil case lasted for over a year.

Following the acid attack on me in December 2015, I ensured that every daily newspaper in Scotland was aware of the case when it was next called early in 2016. In a memo circulated to editors, I said:

> The acid and knife attack on me at my home came after we published a series of articles about Mr Donaldson. These articles related to two court cases involving him – one civil, one criminal.
>
> In the criminal case, he is accused of threatening to shoot his ex-partner (Jane Clarke) and inflicting years of physical violence against her. She – and other witnesses – have suffered a very serious and ongoing intimidation campaign. These include threats to have acid thrown in her face.
>
> Simultaneously, he is pursuing her through the civil courts for £500k [this later increased to £1million], claiming a stake in her chain of kids' nurseries. I believe that this case merits a united front and as broad coverage by as many newspapers as possible.

If the acid attack was supposed to temper journalistic interest in his activities, then it did not work. In fact, it had the opposite effect, as the press a showed touching unity by simultaneously publishing the story, thereby bringing it to the widest possible audience.

I also ensured that press photographers were present. Two of them – from *The Scottish Sun* and *Daily Record* – joined forces to skilfully capture the first picture of Donaldson for at least a decade.

Even more surprising than suing in the first place was Donaldson's risky decision to give evidence in his mischievous case. He was questioned by Jane's advocate, Jonathan Brown, about the assault allegations but declined to answer as to do so could have incriminated him. When Brown said, 'You will understand, I think, that Miss Clarke's position is she was subjected to sustained violence,' Donaldson's response was that he had 'absolutely nothing to say'.

During one exchange, he claimed not to know one of his children's date of birth – to the incredulity of Sheriff Anthony Deutsch. When the sheriff asked him to explain how he had arrived at a sum of £80,000 which he claimed to have initially invested, Donaldson blustered, 'I can't remember what I done last week never mind 15 years ago.'

Donaldson also talked about his previous business relationship with mortgage broker Iain Mulholland, the brother of Frank Mulholland, at the time Lord Advocate, in relation to a Dubai property transaction. Donaldson's evidence was inconsistent, with shades of contempt, bordering on farcical. The only person who supported his purported involvement and financing of the nursery chain was his friend Colin McGowan, the chief executive of Hamilton Accies FC who has spoken at length about how drugs and alcohol addiction destroyed his own youth. The next of his witnesses due to be called was convicted fraudster turned millionaire property developer

Bill Roddie. But, thankfully for Roddie, he didn't have to appear as Donaldson suddenly abandoned his case.

Jane was relieved. Due to the intimidation campaign, she had been granted the right to testify from behind a protective screen, but the prospect of being forced to counter outrageous lies cooked up by a man who had physically battered her countless times was daunting. Had the case proceeded, the court would have heard more lurid details of Donaldson's violence and his complex and international financial affairs. To have embarked on the case was reckless, but Donaldson exhibited some sense in quitting before it got any worse. His lawyer did not even attempt to challenge Jane's request that he pay all costs for his absurd legal action. Whether Jane's legal bill is ever paid by him remains to be seen.

The purpose of the civil case had been to crank up the pressure on Jane, to wear her down and to break her. All the while, she was bombarded with innumerable terrifying text messages day and night, all of which were reported to the police and all of which came from untraceable pay-as-you-go mobiles. She was once greeted by a pair of gang-land thugs after she came through arrivals at Glasgow airport. On other occasions her home and vehicles were vandalised. The police installed a panic alarm in her home which would trigger an urgent response, and she was warned to vary her daily routine to make any attack more difficult to plan. One Christmas the threats were deemed so serious that she and her relatives were forced to stay indoors with a police guard outside the property and armed officers circling the area.

There were occasions where she buckled under the immense weight of it all. The temptation to make it all stop was often overwhelming, but she did not break. The civil case served another purpose, and that was as yet another excuse to churn the criminal case. Donaldson's lawyer argued that his trial could not possibly proceed while the civil case rumbled on. The twisted reasoning was that Jane and her sister Liz had conspired to invent the history of violence as part of a financial extortion attempt being perpetrated against him. It was as cowardly as it was fictional.

This is an example of one of the dozens of ugly texts Jane received:

> Tell the polis the truth u robbed the man for years and now ur fittin him its a shakedown and a fit up an ur the lowest ae the lowest horr cunts but yer nt gett away wae it u jist a daft wee lassie and try to kid all but u no kiddin any 1 biggest slag goin and u puttin that wee boy thru it wot u all aboot whatever coming u way u des slag.

During this period, Donaldson was defended in the criminal case by Gordon Jackson QC, a former Labour MSP who has since been elevated to the influential post of Dean of Faculty of Advocates. Jackson got a right result for Donaldson. During one of the countless procedural hearings, the eminent criminal lawyer persuaded Sheriff Stuart Reid, who has a background in civil law, to throw out the case due to an alleged Crown failure to disclose certain information.

I wrote a story which recorded the development while reflecting Jane's disgust and her resigned lack of surprise at the sheriff's decision. I contacted Judy Ferguson, a director of Scottish Women's Aid, who said:

> For women who have taken action after years of abuse it is heart-breaking and it really destroys

them when they get such negative responses. During the process of seeking a criminal justice response, everyone tells them it's the right thing to do. When something like this happens, it's very harmful for women.

Undoubtedly this also affects other women who are experiencing the same problems. Survivors need to get their day in court and for justice to be served.

Prior to publication of that story, I put the Crown on the spot by asking what they intended to do about it. The unpalatable PR stink of having a thug accused of serious domestic violence being able to use deep pockets and churning to cheat justice may have influenced their decision to do the right thing. A month later, I reported that the Crown had decided to appeal the sheriff's decision. When this appeared in print, Donaldson flew into a rage. He had firmly believed that he had won – that the case was over – but, three months after it had been killed off, senior judges upheld the Crown's appeal and ruled that the sheriff's decision was wrong. The successful appeal caused Donaldson's anger to burn brighter than ever. Just weeks later, fake postman William 'Basil' Burns would arrive at my door with his special delivery.

Even though the domestic violence case was resurrected, many more months had been lost to the appeal process. Victims and vulnerable witnesses were put through additional weeks of torture. Whenever Jane hears politicians or police chiefs pontificating about domestic abuse victims being treated as a top priority, she can be excused for her weary cynicism.

The new court date was set down for July 2016. The case had begun in December 2013. Another five charges were levelled against Donaldson, bringing the total to 16. But, as sure as night follows day, it was inevitable that the trial would not proceed on the scheduled date. Donaldson's appetite for delays showed no sign of abating. Many more long and painful months of uncertainty and threats would be endured by Jane before Donaldson ran out of churn and, finally, was cornered like a rat.

12

SLEEPING POLICEMEN

My flip-flops squeaked and slapped on the wet path as I shuffled through the snow-dusted grounds of a hospital on a bitterly cold and grey December morning.

It was six days after the acid attack and I was trudging to yet another appointment with ophthalmic experts who would switch off the lights, apply stinging little drops to my right eye and peer at my scarred cornea. I was wearing flip-flops because my feet were a mess. The skin had been torn from the tops of most of my toes and the balls of each foot had deep, raw open wounds. At least the sub-zero temperatures were numbing the pain. That's what happens when you have a barefoot boxing match on a monoblock driveway. I had tried shoes and trainers but my socks became welded to the sticky cuts which throbbed with pain. Flip-flops and frozen purple feet were a marginally better option.

Every day since the attack had been chaotic – pinballing between medical appointments, dealing with security measures at my home, discussing the attack with my sympathetic and helpful company management while trying to find time to catch up with well-wishers to impart a template take on the insanity that had invaded my life. Emily Bayne of my HR department was a star as she handled the unusual circumstances with compassion and aplomb.

Christmas Day had been quieter and slower than the previous 48 hours but still did not feel anything like normal. I was absolutely exhausted.

My feet had been neglected because the immediate focus had been my burnt eye and face but, after my flip-flop hike, I accepted they would not heal through will-power and fresh air alone. I attended another hospital's out-of-hours GP service where they were cleaned, soaked with iodine and wrapped in bandages. To walk back outside with my feet cocooned in bandages, socks and loose-fitting trainers was blissful.

Later that day, my daughter and I escaped jabbing umbrellas of dreich city streets for the inky comfort of a cinema where she chuckled at an animated movie while I mostly dozed. With my aching, tired eyes rested shut and my phone turned off, the peace and quiet allowed me time to clear my head and think. It had been exactly a week since the attack and I was becoming increasingly puzzled.

My immediate statement to the CID and the photo-graphing of my injuries the following day had been the full extent of my involvement with the police. There had been no subsequent questions from them about who William 'Basil' Burns may have been working for. There had been no questions about which organised crime bosses I had recently written about. Nor were there any questions about which criminals might harbour a particular grudge towards me. Most curious of all was the complete lack of police curiosity about whether any potentially significant information about the attack might have reached my ears, which it had and continued to do.

I assumed that Partick CID officers were busy dealing with Burns. Despite his capture at the scene being a

Christmas gift for them, Detective Sergeant Craig Warren would still have plenty to do with checking phone records and CCTV, building evidence against the getaway driver and chasing down potential witnesses. But surely someone in Police Scotland was looking beyond the bungling hitman? Surely they were as keen as me to establish who had sent him?

I appreciated that no one had been killed – thanks mainly to luck and the hitman's incompetence – but this was a highly unusual case. Not only had there been meticulous planning involved, but the use of sulphuric acid as a weapon, while still a relative rarity, was extreme and disgusting. What truly set it apart was that I was not some two-bob Glasgow hood involved in a feud and who would not co-operate with the police but an honest, fair-minded journalist, targeted simply for doing my job. A bold and audacious attempt on a journalist's life at a family home should have set alarm bells ringing in the minds not just of senior police officers but of politicians too.

For the police to shrug their shoulders, as they appeared to be doing, would be to send a message to Organised Crime PLC that going after the press is no big deal. The moment gangland hits on the media are treated just like everyday incidents, anyone who cares about what type of society we live in should worry. I didn't want any kind of special treatment but, in the darkened cinema, I concluded that attacking journalists should be seen as a clear red line by crime bosses, no matter how slighted they may feel about media attention.

Yes, Veronica Guerin had been murdered by Dublin criminals, and five years later in Northern Ireland a Loyalist gang shot dead the brave investigative journalist Martin O'Hagan, but these types of attacks are mercifully rare in Western Europe. This is Scotland, not some basket case ex-Soviet republic – the type of gangster state where life is cheap and journalists are fair game.

The next morning was the last day of 2015 and I was keenly aware the police were not intending to come to me, so I would need to go to them. Unable to get hold of Warren, I put a call in to the press office, whose diligent staff field all types of media enquiries from the banal to the extraordinary. I asked them if they could get a message to whoever was dealing with the investigation about who was *behind* the attack – that is if there even was such an investigation. Within an hour, an anonymous call flashed up. It was Detective Superintendent Stevie Grant, head of CID for Greater Glasgow, a sprawling beat serving a population of 770,000.

After I'd explained my concerns, he invited me round for a chat. No time like the present, he suggested. Half an hour later I was sitting opposite Grant in his office in Govan. Gruff and to the point but listening and alert, he was the embodiment of a tough CID man. With a nose seemingly flattened by a shovel, there was no doubt that he could put the frighteners on any snivelling wide-boy with an aspiration to gangsterism.

I told him all about my journalistic jousts with Frankie Donaldson and Barry Hughes – the news stories, the legal threats, the odd incident in Sainsbury's and other detailed information, including the revelation that Donaldson wrongly believed I was in a relationship with his battered ex-partner Jane Clarke. I explained why the 'Wee Jamie' comment by Burns was a red herring. I provided Grant with the names of people who knew about the specific incidents and issues which I had just described in the impromptu meeting. Grant asked the occasional question but mostly just leaned back in his chair and listened, deadpan, to what I had to say.

When I hobbled back outside and up Paisley Road West towards the city, I felt slightly better at having been listened to, but I was far from reassured, not least because Grant had not taken a single note of what I told him. Surely my information should be taken as a formal statement if there was any intention of broadening the investigation beyond Burns?

When the sun came up on the first day of 2016, I did not expect an immediate response from my previous day's visit to the CID chief. But, as more days passed and people shook off their festive lethargy and returned to the routine of work, there was still nothing. The only significant development was a very interesting message I received on 2 January. It did not come from the police, but it was exactly the kind of intelligence that should have been of interest to them. A trusted contact had picked up information from the streets of Paisley, where Burns was widely despised for his bully-boy behaviour. Just weeks earlier, he had been accused of taking a knife across the face of a small-time dealer who was struggling to pay 'tax' on his earnings. When I read the text message from my contact I burst out laughing, utterly stunned at the madness of it. It said, 'That clown Basil has been saying he knows you. He's been saying you phoned him up and started slagging his wife and challenged him to come over. That's doing the rounds in Paisley.'

An embellished version of the same story then came via a phone call. The crazy account being told to Burns's fellow guests in HMP Barlinnie was that not only had I invited him round to my home at 8.30 a.m. two days before Christmas but that I was also blackmailing him, and when he innocently arrived expecting a friendly chat about my evil plot, I ambushed him in my pyjamas with the help of my neighbours. While this baying mob of retired teachers and accountants were supposedly beating Burns to a pulp, I went back inside and put on a pair of sturdy boots that I then used to inflict even greater damage. Burns had been humiliated at being overpowered and detained by a mere journalist he had been sent to maim or kill. Maybe the hitman was guilty of hubris, fuelled by believing stories about his fearsome reputation.

He had to come up with something – and this was it. His fantastical story, surely gold-star material in a prison creative writing group, provided me with some light relief. The thought of me blackmailing him was as laughable as the notion that I would want someone like him within a hundred miles of my home. His story did not address why he had turned up dressed as a postman, armed with a bottle of acid and a knife, just £3.05 in his pocket and no keys of any type. I assumed that Burns's face-saving yarn would stay behind bars, as a harmless bedtime story for gullible Bar-L junkies. Surely, there was no chance that his sober and sensible legal team would swallow it and air it in the High Court when the trial began? Well, you would have thought so . . .

Following my sit-down with Grant, a full week passed with zero communication from anyone in the police. Having spent a long time writing about the police and other public bodies, I knew that the most effective way of jolting them into action is to put something in writing. There is nothing authority figures like less than a clear, sober and polite letter which puts them on the spot and becomes a matter of indisputable record. When the letter is addressed personally to a senior officer or public servant, it gives them no room to wriggle and deny knowledge at a later date. My letter began by sincerely thanking Grant for his time, then reminded him what my overarching concerns were. I wrote, 'My 10-year-old daughter could have witnessed me being murdered and I am determined to see justice done. It is vital Police Scotland and the Crown Office endeavour to prosecute the person(s) responsible for sending William Burns to attack me.' It went on to explain that Donaldson was due to stand trial on multiple charges of domestic violence and that victims and witnesses had suffered an appalling campaign of intimidation. I reminded Grant that I had written extensively and exclusively about both Donaldson's domestic violence criminal cases, which at that stage had been churned for two years, and his £1-million shakedown of his ex-partner Jane.

My letter explained:

> Throughout these proceedings, Ms Clarke and other witnesses have suffered an ongoing campaign of intimidation, thought to be directed by Mr Donaldson, using criminal associates such as Mr Burns. The campaign includes a threat to shoot dead a teenage witness if he testifies and a text threat to throw acid in Ms Clarke's face.
>
> In the weeks prior to the attack on me, Ms Clarke was surprised to be told that Mr Donaldson had formed the false belief that she had developed a personal relationship with me. I have never met Ms Clarke. A reason that Mr Donaldson may have come to his belief is that over the past 18 months I often visited my partner who, coincidentally, lives near Ms Clarke.
>
> On the day prior to the attack, the civil case between Mr Donaldson and Ms Clarke was called at Glasgow Sheriff Court. A reporter, whose identity I don't know, was present. It is Ms Clarke's view that Mr Donaldson wrongly believed this reporter was there on my behalf.

I also told Grant about an investigation I had conducted into a tyre-recycling business called Guinea
Enviro in the city's Maryhill. My story, published nine
months earlier, exposed the company's boss Steven Scott
as a criminal linked to a major drug-smuggling gang. A
police operation had resulted in the seizure of £7-million
worth of cocaine and cannabis and 17 of the gang's members being jailed for a total of 63 years. Scott, jailed for
12 months for having a gun, was of great interest because
of a recent trend of major organised criminals moving
into environmental businesses such as recycling, often
being attracted by obscenely generous state subsidies.
The story included a picture of Scott's partner, who was
also his business partner, pouting with a bottle of Dom
Pérignon champagne, and compared him to US TV Mafia
boss Tony Soprano, who ran a 'waste management' business. The story quoted an anonymous source who said,
'He [Scott] owns the tyre business which is clearly very
lucrative but he had a fall-out with his main associate and
has been looking over his shoulder recently.' I explained
to Grant that the story had been unable to identify Scott's
associate as Donaldson. This was due to Donaldson's
ongoing domestic violence case, which protected him by
preventing us from publishing any potentially prejudicial
details such as his involvement with Scott. It was another
example of contempt laws serving to protect a criminal
from legitimate and responsible media coverage.

The letter went on to explain that I had also written
extensively about Donaldson's associate Hughes – including the 'GIRL POWER' story about him and his wife Jackie
which had triggered the 45-minute phone rant to my editor. I also gave details of Hughes coming into Sainsbury's
and eyeballing me a year before.

Finally, I provided the names of two witnesses who
had each agreed to provide a statement to the CID, and

13

SECURITY WARS

Journalists gawped in disbelief, their eyes transfixed on TVs dotted around the silenced newsroom. America was under attack – the Twin Towers had fallen. As I watched intently with *Sunday Mail* colleagues, the news editor interrupted with an order to fetch my passport and get to New York. I only got as far as London. When photographer Henry McInnes and I landed at Heathrow, all US airspace was shut down and every passing hour brought more flightless passengers into the increasingly chaotic airport. By the time the skies reopened two days later, we would have reached Manhattan too late for a Sunday newspaper deadline. Back home, drained and frustrated, I took consolation from an exclusive phone interview with a Glaswegian woman who made a dramatic escape from her 60th-floor South Tower office.

I was in my twenties when I returned to the *Sunday Mail* on the cusp of the new millennium, and every week was different. One Saturday, I was dispatched on a 'death knock' to the home of a pilot who had been killed in a plane crash. I left with a tear in my eye and a notepad full of loving eulogy from the pilot's widow, delivered while her young children played obliviously at her feet. I returned to the office with a framed photo of the wife alongside her husband in a cockpit. My news editor exclaimed, 'Phwoooaarrr! She's alright, eh?' I mumbled that his comment was somewhat inappropriate, but this was met with the indignant response, 'What? She's single, isn't she?

There were rare showbiz forays, such as when the mother of actor Robert Carlyle spoke to me about their 30-year estrangement. Following publication of her plea to repair their relationship, he told *FHM* magazine: 'Any journalist does that to me again, I'll have them. And I'll go to jail for it.' Once he had calmed down, he would hopefully have accepted his mum was entitled to speak and only did so after his public statement that he 'considered her dead'.

Young journalists may aspire to the perceived glamour of showbiz or reporting big global events like 9/11, but my real job was to get my hands dirty by unearthing stories that people would rather stayed buried. There is some received wisdom in Scottish newspaper management that 'crime sells'. Apparently, readers have a limitless appetite for tales about drugs gangs, underworld hits and so-called 'Mr Bigs'. For many years, many of Scotland's newspapers peddled a romanticised fairytale of Arthur 'The Godfather' Thompson as an omnipotent Mr Big with an iron rule over Glasgow's mean streets. On one occasion, Thompson granted an interview to a wide-eyed *Evening Times* pup to announce his 'retirement' as if he were a football manager or MP instead of a common criminal with a few quid and bent detectives in his pocket. After Thompson's death in 1993, much subsequent reporting offered no meaningful insight into the rapidly changing and increasingly sophisticated criminal landscape. The phrase 'organised crime' was not in common use. There was little public awareness of the staggering sums of money being generated by large numbers of smart, ruthless and anonymous gangs leeching the lifeblood of society.

For decades, every single penny made from drugs, vice, fraud, robbery and other crimes was effectively already 'clean', without today's need for laundering. As late as 2003, following the acquittal of a lawyer who had offloaded a drug-dealer client's assets, I reported that there had still not been a single conviction in Scotland for money laundering. Criminals built fortunes with impunity thanks to the failings of the police and complacency of the Crown Office. It was institutionalised incompetence.

You did not need to be an eagle-eyed journalist to realise what was going on. Growing up in middle-class suburbia where drug money was hidden behind gated driveways, it was evident to me that things had moved on from the 1990s and hoary old tales about 'The Godfather'. I did not seek out organised crime. But someone had to do it.

One of the first stories I did of this type featured self-styled gangster Frank Carberry, who ran a security firm which was essentially a protection racket with some letter-head paper and vans. Carberry was feuding with former police officer-turned-fraudster Paul Johnston, who ran a rival firm that used other gangsters to win contracts by making offers that could not be refused. In early 2000, Carberry's secretary allegedly swiped some of his money and sold his company behind his back to arch-rival Johnston. Their dispute became newsworthy when the secretary did a runner to the USA with her new love, Steve 'The Crocodile' Fitch – a convicted killer and minder to rapist boxer Mike Tyson when he was in Glasgow for a farcical bout that lasted 38 seconds. This story resulted in Johnston threatening to slash me when we came face to face in a court. After making the threat, he immediately scuttled over to nearby police officers to falsely allege that I was harassing him.

I later learned that Carberry was not only a security industry bully but a predatory sex criminal with a taste for boys and young men. A story written by me in 2003 revealed that he had fled from Spain, where he was accused of a sex attack on a 14-year-old boy. Two years after that, I told how he was on the run from police in Scotland. They eventually caught up with him and he was convicted of sex attacks on males aged 16, 18 and 20, for which he was jailed for five years.

Little did I know that the story involving Tyson's minder marked the beginning of my coverage of Scotland's 'security wars', which featured a cast of major criminals and would run for over a decade. I was also unaware that the Tyson story would become a gateway to much wider organised crime reporting.

I exposed numerous firms which were nothing but fronts for drug dealing and money-laundering. They used shootings and other forms of violence to force terrified construction firms to buy 'protection'. Thugs on the pay-roll forced clean rivals to quit by terrorising them. The legitimate firms had no way of competing with crooks who failed to pay taxes or the minimum wage. Exploited guards earned less per hour than a city-centre parking meter charge and would be left to shiver in unheated building- site cabins for 72-hour shifts, kept awake by the local young team trying to set fire to it.

The security wars made the 1980s 'Ice Cream Wars' – in which drug gangs fought over Glasgow's ice-cream van routes – look like child's play. It was organised crime on a large scale involving the who's who of the underworld, yet most of the press were not interested. The mentality appeared to be that if something was not handed out in a police press release, then covering it was too much like hard work. More difficult to understand was why the police remained aloof and uninterested in what was going on while MSPs at Holyrood just gazed at the pretty views from their thinking pods.

Frustrated at ploughing this lonely furrow, I contacted fearless BBC reporter Sam Poling, who went undercover to produce a compelling investigation into the security wars. It finally forced the police and politicians to shake off their lethargy and start getting tough on the seedy protection rackets that had been allowed to thrive unchecked across central Scotland for too long. Real action was only taken when firebombing became commonplace, putting innocent lives at risk, and one mob crossed a line by offering 'security' to residents of a housing estate hours after it suffered a mysterious spate of vandalism.

Late in 2000 I went to meet a contact in the Off the Record pub which was close to the old *Daily Record* building and, like the other nearby newspaper drinking den The Copy Cat, is now demolished. A buff A4 envelope was pushed across the small round table. Inside was a police mugshot of Tony McGovern. I smiled with gratitude and made my way back to the office.

McGovern was a drug-dealer whose family operated from the city's Springburn area, where they styled themselves the 'McGovernment' – not that many outsiders would know it because of the lack of any press coverage of their activities. That changed in September 2000, when McGovern, aged 35, was shot dead outside the New Morven pub. His bulletproof vest was not enough to save him from five close-range rounds.

A contact with a deep knowledge of the McGoverns told me an incredible account involving the murder victim, his best friend Jamie 'The Iceman' Stevenson, a family feud and a host of other colourful characters. I published a story explaining how Stevenson and McGovern had fallen out with Tony's brother Tommy but that a peace deal was then struck between the siblings – on condition that Stevenson should be killed. When Stevenson learned of this betrayal, he was not best pleased and a number of tit-for-tat shootings ensued until it was game over for Tony McGovern. Stevenson was arrested and charged but the case was dropped by prosecutors due to lack of evidence and remains unsolved to this day.

I got a phone call from what was then called the Serious Crime Squad, who asked me in for a meeting. Once there, I was surrounded by serious men in Ralph Slater suits who explained that they had intelligence that my life was in danger. I'd upset the McGoverns and I should heed this as an official warning. 'Any advice?' I asked. 'Er, look in your rear-view mirror and go round roundabouts a couple of times.' My boss was less than reassured by the police's safety tips and insisted that I check myself in a hotel for the night.

I was already becoming increasingly aware of protecting my personal information and stayed off the electoral register for years, willing to sacrifice my right to vote in order to make it harder for people to find me. The hotel stay and my own measures were something, but it was obvious that they would do nothing to stop anyone with serious intent.

The incredible McGovern blood feud and Stevenson's subsequent rise, then demise, which saw him jailed for almost 13 years for money-laundering, became the subject of my first book, *The Iceman*, which I co-wrote with then *Sunday Mail* deputy editor Jim Wilson.

The McGovern murder was fascinating for many reasons. One of the most interesting aspects was the drug-dealer's unlikely bond with David Moulsdale, who built the Optical Express retail chain from scratch to become one of Scotland's richest men. I was staggered when Moulsdale's PR man admitted that Moulsdale planned to attend the forthcoming funeral. He told me, 'If David can move his diary about he will be at the funeral. He's known Tony McGovern for many years.' I also found out that another intended funeral attendee was ex-Scotland and Celtic footballer Charlie Nicholas, also a surprising associate of McGovern. As it turned out, Moulsdale and Nicholas did not show face at St Aloysius Church, Springburn.

The *Daily Record* struck a tough tone for its funeral coverage with the headline 'HOODS WEEP FOR SCUMBAG DRUG PUSHER'. That and the biting intro, 'Gangsters crawled from the sewers into the sunshine yesterday to honour a drug-peddling scumbag who blighted a generation', generated death threats for the paper's chief reporter, Anna Smith.

As the friendship between McGovern and Moulsdale was revealed, the businessman won a prize at a charity event – to edit the *Sunday Mail* for a day. In its 'Media Diary', the *Observer* newspaper reported:

Fear stalks Glasgow's *Sunday Mail*. The paper ran a top scoop last week revealing that David Moulsdale, founder of the Optical Express spectacles chain, who is worth an estimated £100 million, was to attend the funeral of murdered Glasgow gangster Tony McGovern.

The night before the story appeared Moulsdale won top prize at a charity dinner: 'Be the editor of the *Sunday Mail* for a day'. Does Moulsdale really intend to edit the *Sunday Mail* for a day?

He insists he does, although no date has yet
been set.

Mail staff, including reporter Russell Findlay,
who wrote the McGovern story, are anxiously
awaiting his arrival. 'Maybe he could be the editor
on Monday – that's our day off,' one staffer said.
'I'll be calling in sick that day,' another added.

Moulsdale, not being accustomed to such lurid publicity,
never did take his seat in the editor's chair and stuck to
selling spectacles and laser treatments.

One unusual aspect to the McGovern case was that not
a single photo of him had been published by any newspaper. The family had ordered the police not to release
one, as is standard in high-profile cases where public
pleas for information and witnesses are sought. It was two
months later that I received the call telling me to attend
Off the Record, where the colour shot of McGovern was
handed over.

Writing about the security industry continued to yield
information about other criminals. They included Paul
McGovern, a younger brother of Tony and Tommy, who
set up his own firm after being released from prison
where he did time for murder. Another security firm villain was Robert Wright, from Blackburn, West Lothian,
who I revealed was wanted in connection with a multi-
million-pound heroin bust in Estonia. He spent five years
fighting to avoid extradition to the Baltic state but was
eventually jailed – despite the best efforts of one freelance journalist who planted stories in newspapers about
the supposed unfair treatment of Wright and his drug-
smuggling sidekick Les Brown. When Wright later came
home, almost inevitably he returned to the security game
and, despite his heroin-smuggling conviction, his firm

managed to win contracts with an English police force and large, respectable businesses.

Yet another crook involved in security was Lewis 'Scooby' Rodden, who first came to public notice in 2001 when he was shot in a strip club in Amsterdam while in the city to watch Celtic play. The non-fatal shooting was allegedly ordered by a wealthy industry rival who had done very well for himself, helped along by being a police informant, according to his enemies. The most astonishing aspect of the Amsterdam shooting was that photographer Alan Simpson and I were dispatched there by the *Sunday Mail* while our sister title, the *Daily Record*, also sent a two-man team. The same newspaper company flew four employees to Amsterdam, put them up in nice hotels and paid their expenses when two could have done the job for both titles. The accountants would have twisted a few paperclips in fury that day.

While the *Record* duo careered around the city trying to find the shooting victim, we did the same, ending up staking out a hospital where he was ensconced as a stream of stern-faced Glasgow 'businessmen' came and went. That night, as the four of us compared notes over Amstel and Heineken, we knew that the days of editors being allowed to spend so freely were coming to an end. Today, to the delight of the accountants, it is almost certain that the Amsterdam shooting would be reported from inside the newspaper office with desk-bound staff expected to get their information and images online and via phone calls. A few clicks of a mouse – cheap, sterile, all nice and safe.

14

CRIME INC

Some Scottish Labour politicians happily supped with organised criminals for decades but they did not use a long spoon. It took more than a generation but they eventually paid the price. As political science students theorise on the proud party's sudden and extreme demise, rarely do they seem to dwell on the corrosive effect of the close proximity to gangsters.

In March 2002 perma-tanned, Porsche-driving drug-dealer Justin McAlroy was shot dead in the driveway of his home in front of his pregnant wife. Two *Sunday Mail* colleagues and I wrote a report which explained that McAlroy, aged only 30, had became a high-level dealer with links to the Russian Mafia. Our story stated that 'his list of associates reads like a who's who of the criminal underworld' and listed Stewart 'Specky' Boyd, Jamie Daniel, the McGovern mob, Paisley crook Grant Mackintosh and, of course, the bad penny that is Frankie 'Donuts' Donaldson.

Five days later, veteran journalist Mark Howarth revealed that McAlroy not only chummed about with mafiosi from Moscow but also courted the Labour variety. Howarth's exclusive story told how First Minister Jack McConnell, the country's most powerful politician, 'partied with notorious gangster' McAlroy at a party fund-raising event. McAlroy was shot dead six days after the Red Rose dinner held at a golf and country club, which was then co-owned by his Labour-supporting businessman father, Tommy McAlroy.

McConnell and his wife Bridget posed for pictures with supporters as large sums of money sloshed around. McAlroy Sr paid £500 for a table and £1,200 for a case of whisky. Also in attendance at the Red Rose event were MSP Frank Roy and MP John Reid, who was Northern Ireland Secretary at the time. Reid's Special Branch minders were surely curious about the company being kept.

Howarth's bombshell was buried on page 35 of his newspaper but it released the organised crime genie from the Labour lamp, sparking a slew of over a hundred stories by multiple papers. There can be a tendency in tribal newsrooms to ignore a rival's scoop, which is often short-sighted, as there are occasions where collaboration and unity is the only way to effectively tell a difficult story and maintain pressure on wrongdoers.

I got a tip that McAlroy had been under surveillance by a specialist team of drugs squad officers days before his murder. My story, coming two days after Howarth's, told how the drug squad surveillance op was ordered by another police faction, the Scottish Drug Enforcement Agency (SDEA) but had been called off days before the shooting. A police source told me, 'The SDEA wanted to know why our surveillance guys had been called off the job and why they were not told about it. There's nothing sinister about it because the surveillance teams are very much in demand.' The story also divulged that McAlroy had been questioned by police over the previous year's murders of two other dealers, David Macintosh and John Hall. That double murder remains unsolved.

Information continued to emerge as the dark, con-joined underbellies of Lanarkshire politics and gang-sterism became exposed to daylight. A few weeks later, I reported details of one possible motive for the murder, which was that McAlroy had been caught in the middle of a feud between Donaldson and Boyd, who had fallen out. Such was Donaldson's closeness to McAlroy that they had even been planning to build adjacent houses on country club land owned by McAlroy's father. Donaldson, who never settles at a fixed abode for long, eventually did move there for a spell. The story stated that 'Donaldson is so alarmed at the murder of his gangland ally he is trying to forge new links with other underworld figures'.

A source close to Donaldson told me, 'Justin was killed because of who he was connected to just as much as what he was responsible for. He was out of his depth, a name dropper and an easy target. Getting to him will have shaken his associates, including Donaldson.' It had been a year since the court case over the foiled 'plot to put a hole in Donuts' and here he was again, cropping up at the heart of an extraordinary tale of drugs, murder, money and power. Who'd have thought it? But there was still more. I discovered that McAlroy Sr and his son had been watched during a joint surveillance operation between the SDEA and their counterparts in Estonia. Father and son met security firm boss Robert Wright and his busi-ness partner Les Brown who, by the time of the murder, were two years into an epic five-year battle to avoid being extradited back to the Baltic country, where they were eventually jailed for heroin smuggling. Also spotted at the pow-wow was another Scottish drug smuggler. Perhaps it was a traffickers' convention.

An unexpectedly talkative source at KaPo, the Estonian Internal Security Service, told me, 'McAlroy Sr was seen with Wright and Brown on several occasions. His son was seen on one occasion.' When I sought an explanation from McAlroy Sr, his lawyer said he had been in Tallinn discussing a bakery business with Brown.

Political journalists also joined the Red Rose fray, although their interest lay mainly in anomalies involving the money raised by the black-tie event. Many firms who attended the fundraiser secured contracts from Labour-controlled North Lanarkshire Council, with McAlroy Sr's building company winning work worth £9.3 million.

William 'Tiler' Gage had convictions for violence and firearms and was out on licence when he allegedly gunned McAlroy down in cold blood. He was found guilty two years later and will serve at least 20 years, although he continues to wage a noisy campaign protesting his innocence. During Gage's trial, more details emerged of McAlroy's connection to other high-profile criminals – including my acid attack postman William 'Basil' Burns. The court heard that on the day of McAlroy's murder Gage had travelled to Perth Prison, where he had business to discuss. He visited George 'Goofy' Docherty and Burns, who was then at the beginning of his '15-year' sentence for shooting the innocent female security guard during a robbery.

Nine months after the Red Rose dinner, McConnell admitted that he had also been gifted membership of the golf and country club near Motherwell.

The former treasurer of McConnell's local Labour Party was eventually convicted of embezzling £11,000 from party funds while the First Minister was cleared of any wrongdo-ing, but the stench was not easy to banish. For anyone living in rotten borough heartlands such as Glasgow, Lanarkshire and Renfrewshire, Labour's red rose long exuded a less than sweet scent.

The Red Rose dinner was of keen interest to police chief Graeme Pearson, who later headed the Scottish Crime and Drug Enforcement Agency (SCDEA), formerly the SDEA. Pearson later became a Labour MSP and was exactly the sort of clean and straight-talking individual the party needed in Scotland as their best talent refused to swap Westminster for Holyrood.

In his autobiography *The Enforcer: A Life Fighting Crime*, Pearson warned of the dangers of gangsters attempting to groom politicians and public bodies. In it, he writes, 'His [McAlroy's] murder revealed the close proximity between the legitimate and criminal worlds in Scotland. Had McAlroy not been murdered a few days later, many people at the event might still be unaware that organised crime was using the event to assess what value this attending could bring to their organised crime activities.' While Pearson is correct to say that the saga only became public due to McAlroy's murder, it still needed Mark Howarth's journalism to unearth the connection, prove it and push it into the public domain. For it to gain traction and widespread public awareness, the story then needed the continued, dogged pursuit by Howarth and other journalists who know a scandal when they smell one.

One difficulty journalists had with trying to effectively investigate Red Rose was that the power of Labour reached deep into the newspaper industry, way above my pay grade. Pre- and post-millennium, Labour held absolute power in virtually every corner of Scotland. The political map was almost entirely red. Many editors were too close to the leading politicians who, in turn, were too close to the newspaper proprietors, while political journalists peddled party spin so effectively that they often ended up jumping ship to join their PR teams.

As leading media commentator Roy Greenslade describes it on a UK level, getting too close to politicians creates 'a relationship corrupted by mutual suspicion and cynicism in which the public have been the chief losers'. When this analysis is applied to small and incestuous Scotland, the clubby nexus between politics and the media becomes even more acute, even more cloying. Any journalist you ask will have anecdotes about valid stories being mysteriously spiked or the most incriminating details neutered by the hidden hands of political meddling. It used to be Labour, now it is SNP.

By any measure, Red Rose was astonishing. An all-powerful political cabal including the country's leader supping with a drug-dealer linked to major domestic cartels and the Russian Mafia. In the US, it would merit a series on Netflix.

But it would be wrong to think that Red Rose was unique. The previous decade had seen Paisley's drugs war featuring senior Labour politicians and the murderous mob of 'Specky', 'Goofy', 'Piggy' and 'Basil'. Paisley North MP Irene Adams had accused a taxpayer-funded security firm, which was staffed by those gangsters and fronted by Labour officials, of involvement in drug-dealing and money laundering. This poisoned the local Labour Party and plunged it into a toxic civil war which led to the suicide of Paisley South MP Gordon McMaster in 1997. He left a note accusing neighbouring Labour MP Tommy Graham of smearing him over an alleged but denied gay relationship. The Labour fiefdom of Renfrewshire had been the setting of a drugs war, numerous murders and an MP's death. Lessons would be learned, the party insisted. Yet a few years later, the stronghold of Lanarkshire had produced the Red Rose scandal which illustrated the real and present danger of civic Scotland becoming corrupted by criminals. This time, lessons would be learned, the party insisted.

Little did I know that another Labour scandal, in the party's dominant power base of Glasgow, was just over the horizon and was about to come my way. The *Sunday Mail* news editor Jim Wilson called a conference with me and two of my colleagues – the paper's chief reporter, Charles Lavery, and news reporter Derek Alexander. Wilson wanted the paper to run a series on crime and was open to ideas about what it should be about. I suggested that it was time to focus on the numerous extremely wealthy organised crime gangs who had never been named by the press. Having already shone a spotlight on the McGoverns following Tony's murder, we should now look at some of the others.

The small team got to work and produced a ground-breaking series entitled 'Crime Inc', the name illustrating how crime had evolved to become slick and professional, like any other type of business involving massive profits. Our team included two photographers who possessed the skill, discretion and vast reserves of patience needed to execute 'snatch photos' of unsuspecting targets, even the type of edgy people who were permanently paranoid about police surveillance and getting photographed. One of the snappers was so adept at taking pictures unseen he nicknamed himself 'the Washington sniper' after the guman who picked off innocent people in the US capital in 2002.

Crime Inc was all about the money. Top of our rich list was the Daniel family, headed by Jamie Daniel. We told how 'as teenagers, they terrorised the streets of Possilpark in Glasgow' but had graduated to run 'the sharpest criminal operation in the country'. The series ran in January 2003 and gave a host of high-level criminals the novel and unsettling experience of having their faces on public display and their assets exposed. Some went running to their lawyers to complain, but we swatted away the irritating and groundless letters of complaint. Almost immediately, the team regretted certain omissions from the rich list but, as long as they were on our radar, their time would come.

By happenstance, at exactly the same time as Crime Inc was running, the Daniels were involved in a drugs war with another criminal family called the Lyons, who had not made our list. One week after exposing the Daniels, we told how they and the Lyons were fighting for control of the drugs trade in north Glasgow, causing a spate of shootings and slashings. That story prompted an approach to me by a vocal, plucky and respected community activist called Johnny McLean, who lived in the Milton housing estate where the Lyons were causing mayhem through bullying decent people. McLean told me the head of the family, Eddie Lyons Sr, had successfully inveigled himself into the affections of local police officers and Labour politicians, including Councillor Ellen Hurcombe. Lyons posed as an industrious community leader who only had the best interests of underprivileged young folk at heart. With the support of the police and Labour, he was given the keys to run Glasgow City Council-owned Chirnsyde community centre, ostensibly to help Milton's youth. In reality, Lyons was a Faginesque figure and Chirnsyde was a gang hut for his sons and their thuggish cohorts, who styled themselves the Club Boys. Glasgow is not short of weasel-faced, territorial teen gangs, but they were the first to have the tacit backing of the authorities.

McLean put me in touch with a handful of other brave residents who had suffered threats and intimidation for having the guts to oppose this obscenity in their community. The residents told me how Lyons had been foisted on

Milton after he was stabbed in a previous feud in nearby
Cadder and forced to flee after giving evidence against his
attacker in court. I listened in disbelief as they explained
how an innocent dad had gone to Chirnsyde to plead with
Lyons to stop the Club Boys from terrorising and attacking his sons. The man was ambushed and stabbed by a
mob. He alleged that Lyons shouted, 'Get the bastard!'
during the frenzied and cowardly pack attack. The victim
and his decent and hard-working family were forced to
abandon their homes as the criminal case was marred by
witness intimidation.

I was told that community police officer PC John
Cameron was a friend and supporter of Lyons and even
used Chirnsyde as an unofficial police station, to the
astonishment of the CID officers investigating the stabbing of the dad there.

And finally I was told that all pleas to the area's Labour
politicians – MPs, MSPs, councillors – had fallen on deaf
ears. The residents explained that Chirnsyde was under
the control of Glasgow Life, a council arm's-length body
whose chief executive is Bridget McConnell – wife of Jack.
The campaigners believed that was why the Labour politicians were unwilling to resolve the perverse situation of
Lyons being allowed to groom a teen crime gang while
posing as a pillar of the community. Johnny and the other
residents explained that attempts to generate publicity
had failed because whichever newspapers they spoke to
had their initial interest quickly extinguished by Labour,
the police and the Labour-run council. I told them that
I would give it a go. The plan was to keep it simple. The
Washington Sniper captured a photo of Lyons standing in
the Chirnsyde car park while staring open-mouthed.

The resultant story and snatch picture appeared in
February 2003 under the rhetorical headline 'Would

you let this man look after your children?' It made public how Chirnsyde was bankrolled with £120,000 a year of taxpayers' money while the Lyons family quarrelled with the Daniels. It was the first of hundreds of stories about what became the country's longest running gang war. As the McConnells were friendly with senior executives in my company, I was unsurprised when Bridget's name was excised from the story. Councillor Hurcombe robustly defended Lyons with a diatribe which culminated with her saying, 'This is a vendetta against one person [Lyons]. There's no violence in Chirnsyde.' It was quite clear that Lyons was going nowhere – not when he had the backing of Labour and the police. It would take a series of extraordinary events and almost four years of stoic determination by the residents before good finally prevailed.

My attention was beginning to annoy the Lyons. On one occasion, the entire gable end of a tenement block in Possil was spray-painted in foot-high yellow letters with a charming message, with reference to female anatomy, which is too explicit to repeat here.

During that long slog, a council press officer sneeringly branded the residents who were standing up to organised crime as 'the four bampots'. One of these residents, Alex O'Kane, has more integrity in his little finger than the entire sorry shower who protected Lyons. I charted every move of the Chirnsyde scandal and the associated Daniel versus Lyons drug war, which has escalated and continues to this day. The feud led to unprecedented atrocities being committed by both sides: the desecration of a child's gravestone; stolen British Army guns being used in a shooting spree; an assassination at Asda in front of terrified shoppers; the shootings of dads picking up kids at primary school gates; and countless other despicable acts.

Throughout this period the same old gangland names cropped up, as they drifted from one shocking episode to the next. If Scotland's media and political scene resembles a small town, then the underworld is a village.

Having already written extensively about security wars and Tony McGovern's murder, I was becoming synonymous with crime reporting. Crime Inc, Chirnsyde and the Daniel versus Lyons drug war cranked it up further and cemented my name with the genre.

Writing about organised crime was just one of my many areas of interest, and I did not appreciate being pigeonholed, but I could understand why it happened. Unlike some other journalists, I did not treat criminals as celebrities, nor would I allow myself to be used by them. I joyfully went for the jugular and relentlessly exposed new faces to readers. In particular, I doggedly pursued gangster links to legitimate spheres such as politics and the law. And every time we served up a freshly landed crook, it would generate yet more information about other gangsters in need of some attention.

15

PR PLOD

As Sir Robert Peel gazed upon Glasgow's George Square from the granite plinth where he has stood since 1859, he could have been forgiven for shaking his bronze head in bemusement at events below.

The statue of the father of British policing remained still as Deputy Chief Constable Campbell Corrigan posed, his arms folded and looking quite pleased with himself, alongside 13 luxury cars sporting registrations shouting 'Seized!' The press and TV crews were told the array of gleaming Range Rovers, BMWs, Audis and Mercedes worth £350,000 had been taken from gangsters using Proceeds of Crime laws and would be sold to help communities scarred by drug dealing. Corrigan announced, 'The good thing is that, at the end of this process, the money that's recovered from the sale of these things will go back into those communities, and they'll fund not only law enforcement but some of the good things that are on the go there.'

Smelling a rat – and being cynically familiar with police and Crown Office spin – I decided to investigate. It took months of journalistic chipping to prove that the police chief and his PR advisers sold the public a pup that day in 2012. I discovered the cars had actually been borrowed from a car showroom. They were 'representative' of the ones which had been sequestered. This minor deception was fair enough. Many weeks later, an uglier fib was exposed. Not one of the cars was sold under Proceeds of Crime laws and not a single penny was recovered for the public. At least two were just stolen property and most were returned to corporate owners such as dealerships and loan companies. The event had been a sham and the TV and press coverage was fake news. The duping of the public lay entirely with the police because the media had taken their word on trust. If only it was a one-off. Some news editors still ask, 'Have the cops confirmed it?' – as if they only ever tell the truth.

My upbringing was more net-curtain suburbia than No Mean City but I had developed an early wariness of the police or, more specifically, the hierarchy's willingness to be not entirely truthful. This view was shaped partly by the teenage experience of my car windscreen exploding in a shower of glass while driving under a bridge only for the thrower's police chief father to make the problem disappear. On another occasion, my father received a call from a senior traffic policeman who told him a recently issued speeding ticket would vanish because his son was a school friend of mine. When I became a journalist, these suspicions crystallised as I began to see a broader and more vivid picture of police corruption – some minor, some pathetic and some downright chilling. Let's look at the lighter stuff first.

In 2001 a contact offered me a tip that seemed ridiculous. A senior police officer was supposedly driving around Fife displaying some kind of Nazi registration plate on his car. Chief Inspector Robin Lumsden was an avid collector of Gestapo daggers, SS death's head badges, Hitler Youth uniforms and other vile Third Reich paraphernalia.

While the tip about the registration sounded implausible, it needed to be checked out.

Edging slowly through Glenrothes police station car park, there it was – an ordinary car bearing the registration of N5 DAP. The plate represented NSDAP, the initials of Hitler's Nationalsozialistische Deutsche Arbeiterpartei, more commonly known as the Nazi Party. Upon being challenged in his driveway at home, Lumsden dismissed the plate as a 'private joke' and a 'humorous thing'. Whether Fife veterans who fought the Nazis or the families of those who never came home from the Second World War shared Lumsden's mirth was moot. The police decided to back Lumsden, despite criticism and concern from Jewish groups and antiracism campaigners, who branded it 'grossly offensive'. Nothing to see here, the top brass sniffed; it was 'a personal matter'. I refused to let it drop and continually asked for the outcome of an investigation into the Lumsden affair. More than a year later, the police grudgingly told me that he 'has disposed of the plate'. End of story, they bristled. So it seemed, and so they hoped.

But five years after I got a second tip that Lumsden had not 'disposed' of his prized registration as the public had been explicitly told. To my incredulity, he was hinting online that the plate would be rightfully returned to him following his imminent retirement from the police. He was also using the seller name of N5 DAP to flog Nazi tat on eBay. When questioned, he defiantly admitted his intent, prompting the *Dad's Army*-inspired headline 'WHO DO YOU THINK YOU ARE KIDDING, MR LUMSDEN?'

Lumsden's act of apparent provocation was enough for the DVLA to remove the plate from circulation after being lobbied by Michael Matheson, an SNP MSP who later became justice secretary. The DVLA's bold action made a mockery of Fife police's 'personal matter' hand-washing six years earlier. Since Police Scotland's inception in 2013, there have been concerns about the centralisation of local policing, but the N5 DAP debacle illustrates how a small and insular force like Fife could close ranks, dodge accountability and stubbornly defy common sense.

Even more bizarre than the Nazi tip-off was a call I got telling me that a male police officer from Maryhill was a prostitute in his spare time – one of the benefits of shift work, I suppose. My contact directed me to a website where Master Rajj, wearing crotchless leather trousers and a studded cap, advertised his services to other men for £100 an hour. His advert stated, 'The leather pictures are all I have at the moment so if you're not into leathers don't just ignore me, send a message to me, I don't bite!!! Aarrr.' I phoned Master Rajj, who agreed to bring another male escort chum for a three-way session at an Ayrshire farmhouse. He offered to dress as a doctor, soldier or priest. This couldn't really be a cop, could it? But it was. Master Rajj was the *nom de guerre* of a married police officer who was a poster boy for ethnic diversity in the ranks. I chose not to keep my appointment at the Ayrshire farmhouse and phoned Master Rajj to explain who I was and that a story about his sordid sideline was to be published. It took more than four years for his case to be investigated and then limp through the tortuous and secretive disciplinary process, by which point he was no longer a police officer.

As well as a Nazi car registration and the fake seized car stunt, stories about boats and the police provided entertainment. One tale involved daring acts of ocean-going adventure on the high seas, or so one police chief wanted the public to believe.

Chief Constable Willie Rae gazed wistfully into the middle distance for press photographers as he stood at the bow of his new toy, a 60-foot vessel called *Gantock*. According to Rae, the boat would be used to fight the scourge of people-trafficking and drug-smuggling apparently plaguing the River Clyde. He didn't go as far as mentioning Somali pirates. Cutting through the spin, I learned that the *Gantock* was an ageing rust-bucket offloaded by her previous owners because of crippling repair bills, and that the crew was actually targeting al fresco alcoholics and naughty children, not Pablo Escobar and Osama bin Laden. One source said, 'They've lifted around a dozen kids playing truant from school and some OAPs on a riverside drinking session. The main occupation seems to be recovering lifebelts chucked into the Clyde by vandals.' The boat problems continued. A year later, they attempted to silence the critics by replacing *Gantock* with a former RNLI lifeboat at a cost of £150,000. But eight months later I discovered that the replacement boat was still in dry dock on the Isle of Wight, where she was undergoing £40,000 worth of repairs.

Another amusing episode was the decision by the SCDEA to issue officers with brass shields, of the type used by the FBI. I first saw one being worn on the hip of an SCDEA PR dude who seemed to think he was starring in his own private episode of *The Wire*, not sending out dreary press releases from an airport business park. An SCDEA annual report stated, 'This is the new logo of the SCDEA. All members of staff are issued with a shield, which reflects the logo, on starting work at the agency.' I spoke to agency boss Graeme Pearson, holder of badge #1, who told me, 'It's an American-style shield. It was a desire to have something that was professional, self evident and something the public would recognise.' Great,

I thought, let's publish a picture of one of these snazzy shields for the public to see the unusual new ID being used by undercover officers. After all, some burly bloke in a hoodie and Adidas Sambas flashing a golden FBI badge at a drug-dealer in Possil may not be taken entirely seriously. Perhaps through embarrassment, the SCDEA point blank refused my request. This decision invited obvious criticism, with Lib Dem justice spokesman Robert Brown saying, 'The idea of this badge being kept secret from the public is utterly ridiculous. This seems to be a waste of public money. It sounds like the SCDEA had some kind of *Starsky & Hutch* aspirations.'

Some journalists make a safe living by lapping up sanitised spin from police PR departments. A stock technique is to take a local paper youngster out on a drugs raid which usually secures a front-page headline about the smashing of a major cartel and locking up dozens of its members. These are illustrated with a photo of a half-dressed junkie, milk-white face pixelated, being huckled in handcuffs from his council house. It's low-level nonsense. Most of those arrested are never prosecuted, but the local press don't seem interested in reporting the anticlimactic outcomes. One former 'crime reporter' made a career of passing off police PR as news. Just like 'political journalists' who end up on the payroll of their party masters, he eventually took up employment with the police.

Today, the culture of silly spin is worse than ever. Many journalists have the ability and desire to challenge police spin but they no longer have the time do so as their numbers have been decimated due to the death by a thousand cuts of newspapers.

Exceptional journalists like Chris Musson of *The Scottish Sun* still take the hard route of chiselling away. His valiant quest for truth and transparency often results in police

PR departments making groundless complaints about Musson to his bosses. This, thankfully, only serves to make him redouble his efforts. If only these PR Plods took heed of Sir Robert Peel's famous principles of law enforcement, one of which states, 'To recognise always that the power of the police to fulfil their functions and duties is dependent on public approval of their existence, actions and behaviour, and on their ability to secure and maintain public respect.'

16

THE FILTH

In 1996 a detective searching the empty home of murdered teenager Lawrence Haggart edged into the kitchen
where he caught glimpse of a hammer. Carefully picking
it up with a latex-covered hand, he smiled with satisfaction. Was this the murder weapon? Proof of what some
in CID knew? Lawrence had been bludgeoned to death
and set on fire by a younger brother jealous of his football
talent? No, no, and most emphatically no.

That snapshot moment in an ordinary family home
in Larbert, Stirlingshire, could have resulted in Dennis
Haggart, then aged 12, being framed for murder. If some
CID officers had got their way, this grieving child's life
would have plunged into an unimaginable abyss from
which there would be no way out, and serial paedophile
Brian Beattie would cheat justice. Thank God it did not
come to that.

Following Beattie's eventual conviction, Assistant Chief
Constable James Mackay was ordered to investigate the
CID's conduct. For seven years, only privileged eyes
within the highest echelons of the police were allowed
sight of Mackay's subsequent report. Even Lawrence's
family – distraught, persecuted, smeared and betrayed –
were refused access to it. To falsely accuse an innocent

child of murdering his own brother without a shred of evidence was an outrage. To then refuse to come clean only aggravated that outrage.

I had long been intrigued about what might be in the suppressed report. Then, in 2005, came a possible breakthrough with the advent of the Freedom of Information Act (FoI), which journalists were told would change everything. It was one of the best things Tony Blair ever did. Public sector pen-pushers who treat information about wheelie bins as if they were guarding the nuclear firing codes would be forced, by law, to divulge it when asked. As the years passed, FoI became blunted as the wheelie-bin guardians found clever new ways to twist the law and stymie applicants. In the early days, however, it worked. More often than not, you asked for stuff and you got it.

I decided to seek a copy of the Haggart report, so approached Lawrence's dad Larry and submitted an application on his behalf. When it arrived, it made my blood run cold. Lawrence was murdered overnight on 16 March 1996. The report revealed that his house had been searched a total of nine times when the hammer was discovered on 22 March. Officers who searched the kitchen on 18 March were adamant the hammer had not been there. Within hours of the murder, the police questioned but released Brian Beattie without even checking his alibi. My story in the *Sunday Mail* began by explaining that Mackay's report 'claimed detectives faked diaries and planted evidence in a bid to frame a 12-year-old for the murder of his older brother' and that some officers' conduct was allegedly criminal.

The Haggart case should be taught at Police Scotland's training centre at Tulliallan to every rookie police officer in Scotland. If it deterred just one young detective who thinks bending facts to fit a favoured hunch is an acceptable part of the game, it would be worthwhile. Interestingly, and inexplicably, not a single newspaper or broadcaster followed up the damning contents of the Mackay report. The police force responsible was Central Scotland, a small entity whose size was seemingly detrimental to its effectiveness, especially in relation to large, high-profile cases.

The same applied to the even smaller and more incestuous Dumfries and Galloway Constabulary, whose senior officers were aware of numerous allegations of rape against their colleague Adam Carruthers. They responded to the rape claims by continually shunting him off to new pastures and, for good measure, promoting him to the rank of inspector. The complainers were dissuaded from making a fuss.

Following his eventual imprisonment for rape in 2001, I published a story raising questions from politicians about whether Carruthers' suspected Masonic membership may have afforded him protection by his fellow brethren in Scotland's smallest force. The questions were never answered. At least Carruthers was convicted. A common theme of the most serious cases of police corruption is the tendency to close ranks, to cover up and steadfastly deny any wrongdoing, no matter how blatant or abhorrent.

The Haggart scandal was the worst I came across, but there were rivals in the depravity stakes. In 1997 a newspaper ran a story about PC John Watters, who had been suspended on full pay for almost two years. Headlined 'SCANDAL OF SCOTS STAY-AT-HOME COP', the sympathetic yarn stated, 'He was charged with assaulting and robbing an old couple. But despite all charges being dropped, police top brass have refused to allow him to return to the beat. Instead of being allowed to do the job he loves, he spends every day walking his dog.'

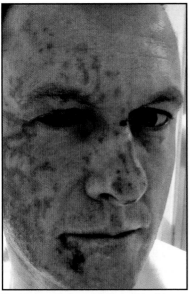

Burn injuries on the face and right eye of journalist Russell Findlay, days after being attacked with sulphuric acid on his own doorstep by a gangland hitman.

Sometimes raking bins is part of the job. Findlay looks for evidence to track down a runaway crook who had ripped off readers of the *Sunday Mail*.

In 1996 Findlay goes undercover inside the former Ravenscraig steelworks in Motherwell to investigate claims that rogue security guards helped gangs of metal scavengers.

The only occasion that a photo of Findlay, then aged 21, appeared in a newspaper. An undercover sting exposed a crooked housing official selling tins of EU beef which were meant for the needy.

A police mugshot of career criminal William 'Basil' Burns, the hitman who came to Russell Findlay's door while disguised as a postman and hurled acid into his face.

The alleged getaway driver in the acid hit, Alex Porter, whose DNA was found on the steak knife carried by Burns. (Spindrift Photo Agency)

Ross Sherlock, an ally of the Daniel organised crime gang, was shot outside a suburban primary school. William 'Basil' Burns was later acquitted of the non-fatal shooting.

A police officer outside the home of Findlay carefully bags the Royal Mail jacket and other items worn by Burns during the botched acid attack.

Frankie 'Donuts' Donaldson, a millionaire with extensive gangland connections, outside court after a hearing into his £1 million claim against ex-partner Jane Clarke. (Mirrorpix)

Donaldson socialising with Bobby Kirkwood (left), an associate who was once jailed for taking a power drill to the head of a gangland rival.

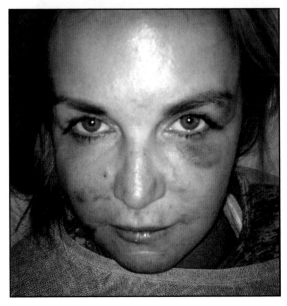

A rare photo of Jane Clarke's injured face after a violent attack in Majorca by her then partner Donaldson. She also suffered bleeding on the brain.

Self-styled tycoon Barry Hughes and his wife Jackie enjoy the high life in Dubai weeks before he was bankrupted owing almost £10 million to HMRC.

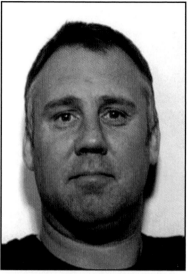

Jamie 'The Iceman' Stevenson, one of many major organised crime figures who has received attention from Russell Findlay and other journalists.

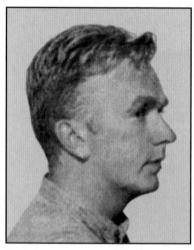

Drug dealer Tony McGovern was shot dead in 2000. Former best friend Stevenson was prime suspect for the unsolved murder.

The 2002 murder of drug dealer Justin McAlroy led to the exposure of murky connections between the criminal underworld and the Scottish Labour party.

Above. Highly-dangerous gangland thug George 'Goofy' Docherty, loyal brother-in-law of Frankie 'Donuts' Donaldson. His 2006 murder is unsolved.

Right. Stewart 'Specky' Boyd, an associate of William 'Basil' Burns, led a crime gang linked to at least nine murders during the 1990s Paisley drugs war.

Below. Fame-hungry gangster Paul Ferris (left) and ex-social worker Reg McKay produced a series of books glamorising criminals. (Mirrorpix)

After quitting Scotland, former Celtic owner Fergus McCann was later tracked down in France by Russell Findlay. (Mirrorpix)

When Rangers owner Sir David Murray wielded great power in newspapers, one clash resulted in an editor losing his job.

Police chief Campbell Corrigan shows off expensive cars supposedly seized from organised criminals. But the PR stunt was later exposed as a sham. (Mirrorpix)

Robin Lumsden, a police Chief Inspector from Fife, explained to Findlay that his Nazi-themed number plate was just a 'private joke'.

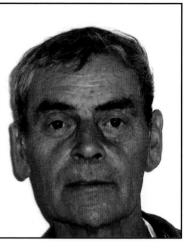

Above left. A police-issued photofit of the elusive 1960s Glasgow serial killer Bible John, who has never been caught.

Above right. Peter Tobin will die in prison for the murder of three young women. Some believe the serial killer is Bible John.

Left. Serial killer Angus Sinclair will also rot behind bars. But did the police give Sinclair a 'license to kill' by fitting up another man for a 1977 murder he committed?

A cartoon by Russell Findlay showing a defence lawyer as a puppet or organised crime with a tendency not to tell the truth.

With Crown Office controversy never far from the headlines, this humorous take on an incompetent prosecutor reflects public concerns.

After being sentenced to '15 years' for the acid attack on journalist Russell Findlay, a cartoon version of 'fat clown' hitman William 'Basil' Burns.

Frankie 'Donuts' Donaldson with a bandaged hand from a street knife attack. He was later targeted again while in prison for domestic violence. (Mirrorpix)

It took 11 years for a somewhat different picture to emerge. A contact who had been part of the investigation disclosed to me astonishing inside information about what he believed had been a fetid cover up. He told me, 'The decision to drop the charges against Watters stank. The top brass were acutely aware of the damage it could do to the force's reputation if the full details emerged.'

Watters was suspected of being a member of a prolific robbery gang whose members included gangster brothers Robert and Raymond 'Rainbow' Anderson, who used police uniforms and fake search warrants to enter houses and tie up victims, who were mostly elderly. Raymond later became a Daniel crime clan hitman who committed one of the most appalling acts in the endless drug war with the Lyons. When I received the tip about the gang, he had just been jailed for using stolen British army guns to attack a Lyons family garage, killing one and wounding two others including Robert 'Piggy' Pickett, best friend of William 'Basil' Burns. Robert was also a pox on society with multiple convictions for violent home invasions and was once cleared of child sex attacks, although his alleged victims were forced into witness protection for daring to speak out.

Watters was a plain-clothes PC in Dumbarton when he was arrested and charged over a robbery in which an 81-year-old man and his wife were tied up and only found two days later. On the night of the crime in Kippen, Stirlingshire, a man was seen in a parked car which was registered to Watters' wife. Watters admitted being there but claimed he was having an affair with a local woman. His alibi was accepted at face value. Police discovered that the best man at Watters' wedding was gangster Walter Kirkwood, who was jailed in Liverpool over guns destined for Scotland. I ordered a copy of Watters' wedding certificate and, sure enough, Kirkwood was a witness.

One crime linked to the gang was the 1995 theft of caps and medals from the Helensburgh home of ex-Rangers striker Mark Hateley. Watters said he could recover Hateley's haul but this was ruled out as the thieves demanded ransom money. None of this information had been contained in the earlier pro-Watters puff piece, planted by the Police Federation's lawyers and which had clearly suited both him and his bosses. I was happy to put that right, even though it was over a decade too late. Yet again, no other media showed any interest in this extraordinary case.

Arguably the most shocking gangland murder in recent years – the slaughter of Daniel mob drug-dealer Kevin 'Gerbil' Carroll – was stained by police corruption and infighting. Carroll was shot dead outside an Asda supermarket in 2010 by two Lyons mob gunmen including Billy Paterson, a 'graduate' of Chirnsyde, the police- and Labour-backed youth club run by Eddie Lyons. Paterson is serving at least 22 years.

Police investigating Carroll's murder found two pages of notes, handwritten by an officer called PC Derek McLeod, stashed in the home of Paterson's girlfriend. The stolen police intelligence charted Carroll's movements, cars and associates and almost certainly assisted the Asda plot. Like Paterson, McLeod also went to prison but the police had absolutely nothing to say about the incredible involvement of one of their own. The ugly saga did not end there. Paterson's alleged accomplice was fellow Chirnsyde alumnus and drug-dealer Ross Monaghan, cleared when his 2012 trial collapsed. The Monaghan trial heard that the leading officer, Detective Superintendent Michael Orr, allegedly put undue pressure on a forensic witness and offered PC McLeod an unofficial deal to co-operate.

Orr was investigated, which resulted in a verbal warning. But he refused to accept it and fought to clear his name – alleging that he had been made a scapegoat. During his long battle, Orr made counter-allegations against Neil Richardson, Deputy Chief Constable of Police Scotland, one of which included a breach of data protection laws for the sharing of a private letter. It took Orr four agonising years to be exonerated. In doing so, he helped expose the relatively new Police Investigations and Review Commissioner (PIRC) as a toothless watchdog – or police lapdog – just as its critics had claimed. PIRC had initially rejected Orr's complaints against Richardson but his detective's tenacity forced them to back down. Orr, a high-ranking officer whose dad was a chief constable and whose uncle was the first head of the SDEA, had the skill and inside knowledge to beat the system. What chance had an ordinary citizen or cop without connections?

Remarkably, the fall-out from Monaghan's botched trial for the murder of Carroll continued to haunt the police. I published two more stories which prompted a chilling new anti-press tactic more typical of tinpot regimes in places hard to find on a map. Both stories featured a variety of allegations against Deputy Chief Constable Richardson – one relating to the Orr saga.

Senior police chiefs thought it legitimate and sensible to unleash a Major Investigation Team (MIT) on me. The job of a MIT is to target serious organised criminals and terrorists. No doubt they were less than impressed at being ordered to go after a journalist for the heinous offence of telling the truth. The deployment of a MIT to intimidate a newspaper and smoke out a whistleblower gravely concerned media experts and free-speech campaigners, not least following the chill winds of the tedious Leveson inquiry. Ex-editor of *The Scotsman*, Professor Tim

Luckhurst of the University of Kent journalism school, told me, 'The allegations published in the *Sunday Mail* plainly deal with serious matters that should be in the public domain. They conform with any serious definition of what is in the public interest. It is alarming that police officers are expending time and energy in an effort to identify the whistleblower.'

To show the police that we would not be cowed, we defiantly responded by publishing a copy of an email from a MIT officer in which he sought assistance from a witness. I half expected a second MIT probe to find out how the hell we got the email. This tawdry saga revealed a series of shocking events that were hugely damaging to public confidence. It exposed how McLeod, a massively corrupt officer, sold at least 18 intelligence logs to a Lyons hit squad. But it also ended the career of Orr, a respected senior detective who was traduced then hung out to dry, and who would have been forgiving had he just been offered a simple apology at the outset.

As well as using terror cops to go after the press, it also exposed how PIRC, the shiny new 'independent' police complaints body, is as byzantine, anti-public and unfair a system as it was when cops investigated cops. *Plus ça change . . .*

And let's not forget, the Monaghan trial collapse had its roots in Chirnsyde – an organised crime gang-hut built with the backing of police officers. There should have been outrage – angry MSPs hammering on the doors of police HQ demanding answers on behalf of the public. Yet, like so many of the most serious scandals, the politicians simply provided a cheap soundbite. It certainly did not help that other newspapers and broadcasters failed to follow up these stories which would have put pressure on the police and politicians. In isolation, they withered.

The same applied to the case of Officer X, a female officer whose identity I agreed to keep secret. The law graduate, in her late twenties, was serving her two-year probation period when she found herself in the peripheral company of known criminals during a night out. Abiding by the rules, she immediately informed her sergeant of the chance encounter. This prompted a routine examination by the police's professional standards unit, which cleared her of wrongdoing. That, she assumed, was that. But a few weeks later the case was reopened. A call had been received by Crimestoppers, the charity-run phone number for tip-offs to the police. To Officer X's disbelief, allegations of consorting with gangsters had been made against her, with just 24 hours of her probation period to run. Her probation was extended and a few weeks later she was served a 'notice of intention to resign' letter – in other words, jump before you're pushed. Confused and emotional, she was forced from her job without any explanation about what had been alleged in the mystery Crimestoppers call.

She told me, 'It was all very vague. I had no idea what they thought they had on me. I was gutted when I was forced to resign because it shattered me and my family. It was such a big embarrassment. No one could believe it. I would never do anything lacking integrity or associate with criminals.'

What happened next was unprecedented. Three months later, she was approached by the police, who sheepishly admitted they had got it wrong and asked her to return. She was given three months' back-pay and a personal apology from Chief Constable Campbell Corrigan – he of fake car seizure PR stunt infamy. She even took her police oath in his private office. The dramatic U-turn had been caused by an investigation into the conduct of one of her bosses, Superintendent Steven Reed, who was suspended from duty and would never return. It was alleged the Crimestoppers call had been false and malicious.

Officer X spent 12 hours being questioned by detectives leading the probe into Reed. She was then told to keep her mouth shut and deprived of any meaningful explanation. Eventually she quit, unable to withstand the whispers behind her back, and only agreed to speak to me anonymously when I tracked her down months later. She said, 'People wanted to know what had happened but I had been told that I wasn't allowed to say anything. They said that was because of the criminal investigation but I think it suited them that this was kept quiet. After everything that had happened, my heart just wasn't in it.' Yet again, this repugnant episode was ignored by other media, which must have delighted the police hierarchy. Pity Officer X, whose career was ruined on a lie.

I went after rogue police officers – and the culture that breeds and protects them – with as much hunger as I chased down and publicly identified organised crime gangs. Following the acid attack, a very senior officer told me that my long history of exposing police scandals would have an inevitable effect on how they treated the investigation surrounding my acid attack. I could not help wondering if this was a coded message. Perhaps I should adjust my expectations and not suppose they would be interested in looking too hard beyond the Christmas gift of William 'Basil' Burns. It made some sense. After all, why would the police, who have very long memories, bust a gut for a journalist who had caused them years of trouble?

There had been the Nazi cop car, the PR stunts, the prostitute PC, the FBI-style shield, the attempt to frame a child for his brother's murder, the robbery gang suspect, the rapist cop, the cop selling stolen intel to a gangland hit squad, the scapegoating of a detective, the smearing of an innocent PC and the use of MITs to investigate me. I could fill many more pages with other such stories spanning more than two decades which would not only add weight to my suspicions but also challenge the comfort-blanket cliché of 'one bad apple' which is trotted out whenever the subject of police corruption arises.

17

THE FERRET

I have a public confession to make. It has eaten away at me for almost 20 years. I alone bear responsibility and seek understanding, if not forgiveness.

Retired social worker Reg McKay asked me a favour – to get him contact details for Paul Ferris so that he could write to him at HMP Frankland where Ferris was doing seven years for dealing in machine guns. The unforeseen consequence of my small act of assistance resulted in the creation of Ferris and McKay – a dubious double act who churned out a series of books glamorising criminals and making excuses for their low-life behaviour.

Ferris came to prominence in 1992 when he was acquitted of murdering Arthur Thompson Jr, the son of crime boss Arthur ('The Godfather') Sr. In revenge for Thompson's murder, Ferris's cronies Robert Glover and Joe Hanlon were shot dead while he was safely tucked up in prison on remand. Ferris wiped away his tears and used the three murders as a springboard to infamy.

After I supplied McKay with the requested address and prisoner number, he reinvented himself. Gone were the Converse boots and scruffy jeans, to be replaced by a black Armani suit and a long funereal coat. Barely a sentence could be spoken without throaty mutterings of 'street players'.

No more touting social work stories to the trade press; aspiring journalist McKay proclaimed that he and Ferris were writing a book. This was not the first time I had seen the phenomenon of gangland groupie. Nor would it be the last. One newspaper reporter became friendly with Ferris but ended up getting too close and was busted by police. Not a word of this was reported in the press.

I watched aghast when McKay, in full *Men in Black* ensemble, drove Ferris from prison in a Mercedes. What had I done? Then came their first effort – *The Ferris Conspiracy*. It was going to name names, they vowed.

Ferris has a brother called Billy. A convicted killer in 1977, he was also found guilty of murdering a child in 2003, for which he will stay in prison until at least 2025. Prior to the release of his wee brother's book, Billy proudly bragged, 'Paul is going to name all the criminals who grassed to police and officers in Strathclyde Police who took bribes.' And name corrupt police officers they did – take that, Detective Sergeant Duff Idle, DS Lonnie Smut, Grady Midden, Greg Diddle and Sweeney Gillette – the only problem being that every single one of them was made up. So McKay's big gun turned out to be firing blanks and failed to level a single allegation against any real people. It was not journalism.

Even worse, Ferris was using the book to hint about getting away with murdering Thompson Jr. He and McKay claimed that a mystery figure called 'The Apprentice' did it. They then revealed details only the killer would know – his state of mind when he shot Thompson and the position of the victim when the bullets struck. And not only was The Apprentice the same age and height as Ferris and from the same part of Glasgow, he was also friends with Hanlon and Glover. To ram home the unsubtle point, the book identifies two other shootings committed by

The Apprentice – for which Ferris was also charged but cleared.

The return of Ferris as a literary equaliser was treated seriously by some newspaper executives who were deaf to criticism about their facilitation of gangster lit. Thankfully there were people like Allan Brown, who wrote in *The Sunday Times* about the release of the pair's second book:

> It will supplement his already published memoir *The Ferris Conspiracy*, perhaps the first book ever to mug its readers, promising to name names, then thinking better of it once the money had been handed over.
>
> Perhaps, though, the real villains are the brokers and the middle-men: the publishers, ghostwriters and critics who regard this literary compost as challenging and instructive. They are salaried cynics, pandering to the literary equivalents of car accident ghouls, perpetuating a cultural practical joke that stopped being funny long ago.

Following his freedom, Ferris became involved in the security industry, just as it was descending into a battle-ground between gangsters. I wrote a spate of stories – perhaps a subconscious seeking of penance for creating the Ferris and McKay double act – about Ferris's involve-ment. These stories included one about his recruitment of a thug with 666 tattooed on his neck whose role was to cover the Dundee end of the expanding Ferris operation. Another told how a dormant feud had reignited due to a turf-dispute and another dusted down his nickname of 'The Ferret', acquired due to his sneakiness, and told how he had been kicked off a site by a bigger, badder criminal who did not sing to newspapers. Yet another revealed that his company was providing security for a new court being built in Dumbarton, all paid for, of course, with taxpayers' money. All of this was set against McKay parroting the line that Ferris was going straight; that he had turned his back on crime.

In 2003 I suggested that the BBC should take a look at security sharks. This resulted in Sam Poling's BAFTA-winning documentary *Security Wars*, which investigated Ferris and others. Poling proved that Ferris was the true owner of a security firm, which he had long attempted to deny.

McKay was now using the sobriquet 'Gutter Sniper' to write a column in *The Big Issue*, whose bosses didn't see the irony in a publication serving the homeless, many the victims of the drugs trade, and giving a platform to an apologist for those involved in organised crime. Beneath a moody photo of himself wreathed in cigarette smoke, McKay described the BBC investigation as 'shabby journalism'.

Beyond his obligatory references to 'street players', 'heavy merchants' and 'faces', McKay expanded on his criticism, which amounted to how terribly unfair Poling's documentary was. McKay also made a few veiled digs at my exposures of rogue security firms in the *Sunday Mail*, which prompted the paper's assistant editor Jim Wilson to write to *The Big Issue*:

> Good crime writing is not easy and I have always tried to defend Mr McKay against persistent criticism that he is merely a 'useful idiot' for a number of gangland figures, most notably Paul Ferris.
>
> However, his posturing as the smoke-wreathed chronicler of the underworld, which has always been faintly risible, is fast becoming offensive.

And for the *Big Issue* to allow him space to defend the reputation of Ferris and his cohorts in the security industry is lamentable.

Unlike Mr McKay's books and columns, our reports are written by professional investigative journalists prepared to risk their own safety to expose violent and dangerous criminals.

Then a very strange thing happened – McKay was hired to bring his 'Gutter Sniper' column to our sister paper the *Daily Record*, where Bruce Waddell had become editor. Thereafter, the *Record* became a temporary conduit for a malodorous slurry of offensive half-truths, lies and threats. This prompted an excoriating attack by Tom Brown, the paper's recently retired political editor and columnist, who commands widespread respect in the newspaper industry. Brown wrote:

How sad it is when you find an old friend rolling around in the gutter with low-life vermin. Even more depressing when they know exactly what they are doing and glorify the scum who make other folks' lives miserable. That is exactly the case with my old paper, the *Daily Record*.

About the *Record*'s decision to serialise the pair's latest book and put Ferris in a TV ad to plug it, he added:

Ferris is a self-styled gangland enforcer, self-confessed junkie, self-pitying long-time jailbird and self-publicising hypocrite, now seeking to make money from his tales of viciousness and violence.

There was a time when no self-respecting newspaper would have given the likes of Paul Ferris a by-line (far less used him in a TV commercial) without thoroughly de-lousing, disinfecting and fumigating the office and all who came in contact with him.

For the *Record* not only to publish Ferris's drivelling self-justification and give it a sympathetic treatment was a gross error of judgement. To use his scarred visage on peak-time Sunday night TV as the face of the *Daily Record* was grotesque.

Even more sickening was the publisher's poster on bus shelters throughout Glasgow, depicting Ferris squinting at passers-by down the barrels of a shotgun. What message does that send?

I read Brown's words with a smile. Our paths had never crossed while working for sister papers but I was moved to express my gratitude. Did Brown's broadside knock some sense into the *Record*? Unfortunately not. For even as I was writing my email to Brown, the paper gave three pages to a *Hello*-style, soft-focus interview with a heroin-dealing Ferris crony. I raised my concerns with a senior *Record* executive who ridiculously replied, 'Hey, big man, it sells papers!' – as if that was our sole purpose. McKay's 'Gutter Sniper' column also remained. One snippet revealed an interesting festive tableau. He wrote:

Over Christmas we had a wee party at our house. Just some family and friends. In one quiet corner sat Tommy Sheridan and Paul Ferris blethering for Scotland. About what?

How to persuade our kids not to carry blades. The feel-good factor will last me to next Christmas.

Hard-left egomaniac Sheridan is the political equivalent of Ferris – a manipulator of the truth who will use anyone to further his own agenda.

The *Record* snapped out of its hypnosis when McKay died of cancer in 2009, leaving Ferris to find a new sympathetic outlet for his wisdom at *The Scottish Sun*.

A year later, I discovered that police attempts to clean up the security industry had failed after courts rejected intelligence reports as grounds to strip licences from those suspected of being puppets for crooks. Detective Superintendent John McSporran alleged that Ferris controlled three firms and told the Security Industry Authority (SIA): 'Ferris is a prominent Strathclyde-based criminal who has attempted to present himself as a reformed individual and legitimate businessman. However, intelligence indicates that he is still involved in serious and organised crime.'

Ferris was obsessed with shaping publicity about himself and I became suspicious of a 'true crime' website because of its pro-Ferris tone and justification of criminality. According to the public record, the site was anonymously owned but I looked deeper to find that a previous owner was a Paisley car valeter living in a Derbyshire spa town. Intrigued, I called the valeter to ask if Ferris was the owner. His garbled response told me everything. He said, 'You want to know who did the site, like, but it's not a big secret. I'll see the lad and see if he wants to, but you're off the ball there – it's not Paul, no. I know Paul, yeah. It's not meant to be secretive – it's just the way it is.'

When the *Sunday Mail* published a story about the website, I immediately became the subject of defamatory comments from internet trolls on another website which did not hide its Ferris connection. Unlike journalists, these people hide behind fake names.

If anyone thought the deification of Ferris couldn't get any worse, they were mistaken. A long-touted film somehow became a reality. Prior to release of *The Wee Man*, which was based on *The Ferris Conspiracy*, I suggested the *Sunday Mail* should revisit his life and crimes to dig out the truth buried under his skyscrapers of fiction.

I tracked down Georgina Russell, the widow of a low-level criminal, Paul Hamilton, who was shot dead in 1993. Hamilton went to his death after taking a phone call from his supposed pal Ferris, whose book peddled a sensationalist and untrue version of the unsolved crime. The widow said, 'Paul's not here to defend any of these lies. No one can justify the killing of someone else. Ferris doesn't know the meaning of truth. It's all the other people who are left behind who pay the price. I don't hate him – I loathe him.'

I also tracked down John Hogg, an innocent man who was accidentally shot in 1984 while walking home from a night out with his wife and friend. The jittery young gunman blasted the wrong man. Ferris stood trial but got a not proven verdict. Hogg welcomed the right to put the record straight after I showed him *The Ferris Conspiracy*, which claimed the masked gunman 'compensated' him for being unintentionally shot and praised his 'honourable' behaviour during the trial. Hogg said, 'That's a pure fairytale. As far as I've heard about the book, it's mostly fiction anyway. There wasn't any compensation or apology. It's a piece of nonsense. The book said the gunman respected my evidence but I went into court and told them everything I knew. I held nothing back.'

Another untruth in the book related to the Paul Hamilton murder. Ferris gloated that the police had questioned him and an associate called Stephen McLaren about the murder, 'before releasing us, never to bother us again'. He added, 'I'm pleased to say that Stephen avoided all bitterness and has gone on to make an honest, trouble-free life for himself.' I established that McLaren had actually been jailed for five years for heroin dealing. The Ferris definitions of 'honest' and 'trouble-free' clearly differ from the dictionary versions.

For good measure, we torpedoed another whopper about Ferris's gangland 'code of honour'. He wrote, 'We don't grass, we don't hurt non-combatants, we do time rather than put our comrades down.' Yet, during his trial for the murder of Thompson, Ferris deployed the defence of pointing the finger at three other men who he named.

When the film premiered in 2013, Ferris basked in the backslapping bonhomie of low-wattage celebrity, but a few bold journalists failed to show the required respect towards this 21st-century warrior poet. Mike Wade of *The Times* captured the tone with his succinct report which began:

> Movie press conferences are rarely as disturbing as the one held yesterday by a notorious Glasgow gangster.
>
> The poisonous atmosphere surrounding Paul Ferris, The Wee Man of a new biopic of that name, was established early when he took exception to the critic who suggested that the film showed that children who are bullied – like Ferris, supposedly – will grow up to be bullies themselves.

Ferris, gazing at his questioner with dead-fish eyes, answered in an 'unnervingly quiet voice' that 'I actually take that as quite an insult'.

When Ferris was asked whether he would tell his young daughter about his criminality, he responded, 'When she is at an appropriate age, of course I would – as much as someone in the Armed Forces. Would they want to talk about their role in Afghanistan or Iraq? Or elderly people talking about the Second World War?'

Marc Deanie of *The Scottish Sun* homed in on this offensive comparison between criminality and armed service for your country. Deanie obtained a damning response from a wounded veteran and the father of a soldier killed in Afghanistan.

Glasgow, like any city, is not short of fizzing little human volcanoes, so what black magic transformed this one into a celebrity? Firstly, in Scotland, real stars are thin on the ground as they tend to escape domestic drizzle for London's bright lights or LA's sunshine at the first opportunity. Into the vacuum step thugs like Ferris and Barry Hughes. Their shtick – bling, fast cars, doe-eyed molls – is not quite stellar but could just about pass for *Heat* magazine fare, if you squinted your eyes a bit.

Another reason is that many west of Scotland men are afflicted with a condition which we will call 'hard-manitis'. Symptoms include being gripped by an irrational and fevered fascination, admiration even, for criminals. The sufferers, otherwise law-abiding and sane, view those like Ferris as cult heroes. Several newspaper executives – they know who they are – have caught extreme doses of this disease. The condition's name comes from the media's description of them as 'hard men' which makes no sense whatsoever because they are, in fact, the complete opposite – weaklings, cowards, sneaks and bullies.

18

DIRTY BRIEFS

A hitman frantically and ferociously ripped his blade into the face and body of Law Society of Scotland Deputy Chief Executive Les Cumming and left him for dead on the pavement in a pool of blood.

Cumming was knifed a dozen times in 2006 outside his home in one of Edinburgh's smarter postcodes. His attacker fled to Australia but was brought back to Scotland and jailed for 11 years in 2011. They got the hitman, but what about the man in the BMW who paid him £10,000 cash?

Cumming's job was to investigate crooked solicitors, and it seems he was a bit too good at it. The Cumming attack was of interest to me because of its extreme and unusual nature. In the immediate aftermath, a whispering campaign was conducted against the naysayers, outsiders who question the sanctity of the precious profession. Arch-critic and legal blogger Peter Cherbi was stunned to learn that a Law Society official was suggesting his possible culpability to disbelieving journalists at *The Scotsman* newspaper. It was a groundless smear against an unsung hero for those fighting against crooked lawyers – someone who has single-handedly brought about judicial reform. The Law Society should have been looking closer to home – to one of their own.

Nine years after the attack, I was told the name of a wealthy lawyer who was supposedly the prime suspect – the mystery man in the BMW. In addition, the same Edinburgh solicitor had been linked to the unsolved murder of Nairn banker Alistair Wilson, who was shot dead on his doorstep 14 months before the Cumming attack.

I tracked Cumming down by phone in January 2015 and, upon putting the name of the lawyer to him, he said, 'He's a name I know. There were two solicitors who were well connected with criminals and he was one of them at the time who was looked at, but obviously nothing more happened from it.' Cumming also revealed to me the hitman had been offered a deal to identify his paymaster but opted to keep his mouth shut. I wrote a story which, for the first time, linked the lawyer to both the Cumming and Wilson hits, although we were legally prevented from naming him. Frustratingly, the story was not published. Just 19 days after my 10-minute conversation with Cumming, he died of cancer. I floated the story again, but there was still no appetite and it was spiked, a decision that still baffles me.

While underworld snakes and naughty police officers are plentiful enough, limitless sleaze and scandal can be found in the teeming swamp of Scotland's legal profession. I have investigated innumerable cases of lawyers causing chaos and blighting lives, leaving bewildered, broke and broken clients. I have sat with poor souls, vast folders stuffed with carefully indexed documents, whose suffering at the hands of a lawyer is exacerbated by the rigged system that protects them. Members of the public need patience, tenacity, brains and possibly divine powers to negotiate the labyrinthine, lawyer-friendly complaints process.

The biggest problem is of solicitors remaining self-regulated. While Cumming was clearly an effective investigator, his employers – the Law Society of Scotland – play a trick on the public. As the Police Federation backs police officers and British Medical Association (BMA) supports doctors, so the Law Society of Scotland protects solicitors. No one would suggest the Police Federation or BMA should investigate public complaints against their members, but that is exactly what the Law Society does regarding lawyers. They somehow continue to get away with this poacher-and-gamekeeper dual role years after the Law Society in England and Wales was stripped of its regulatory powers. You might think the majority of honest and decent lawyers would recognise how damaging the status quo is to their reputations.

The public has no right to know how many complaints are lodged against solicitors or law firms, which works to allow the worst offenders to trade with a clean image when the entire profession knows they are rotten. Rogue solicitors go running to the shadowy Legal Defence Union (LDU), whose website states that 'Lawyers sometimes need lawyers!' The LDU holds closed-door meetings with the Society to discuss how complaints can be 'resolved'. Polite deals result in lesser punishments being imposed, allowing reprobates to keep preying on unwitting clients. Again, the public are not informed of the outcomes. Only the worst cases are 'prosecuted' by the Scottish Solicitors' Discipline Tribunal (SSDT) but the Society's pseudo-court resembles an in-house HR department and adds more years to the tortuous process.

I pursued serial shyster John O'Donnell for more than a decade as he repeatedly dodged being struck off despite £1 million of insurance claims for negligence and multiple findings of misconduct. When this one-man wrecking ball was finally stopped, he flouted the ban by posing as a colleague.

I urged Sam Poling of the BBC to investigate the self-regulation racket, my motive partly being a press aversion to examining the murkier aspects of the legal profession. Like politics, showbiz and sports hacks, journalists who rely on lawyers do not bite the hand that feeds them. Poling assembled a panel of eminent English legal experts to examine SSDT verdicts where solicitors had simply had their knuckles rapped despite findings of dishonesty. Viewers of *Lawyers Behaving Badly* heard them express surprise that miscreants, including O'Donnell, had not been banished as would happen south of the border.

Well-meaning MSPs tried to fix the problem in 2008 by creating the Scottish Legal Complaints Commission (SLCC), but the unintended consequence was an even more complex process with the new body dealing with 'service' issues while the Law Society maintains a grip on misconduct.

If gangsters are society's playground bullies, their lawyers are sometimes the sniggering sidekicks, happy to do the dirty work, if the price is right. I have written about many with convictions such as smuggling drugs into prison on behalf of George 'Goofy' Docherty, hiding a stash of guns for the McGovern gang, multimillion-pound money-laundering and other paper exercises vital for the smooth running of Crime Inc.

Stories about solicitors who have committed other misdeeds are even more abundant. There was the conveyancer who embezzled £1 million from a bank but didn't get his collar felt and was allowed to keep every penny. An Aberdeenshire lawyer had adulterous sex in his office with a domestic violence victim client, yet the SSDT ruled his identity should stay secret to spare *his* sensitivities. We can only hope he does not drop his briefs when the next troubled client enters his office.

Keith Armstrong, a partner of blue-chip Dundas & Wilson, stole secret files from his girlfriend who worked for a rival top firm, then 'fraudulently and deceitfully' used them to bid for a £500,000 public sector contract.

Another evergreen source of scandal is legal aid, which began as a noble ideal in the 1960s but has mutated into a £150-million state subsidy for lawyers and a free ATM for gangsters' legal fees. The annual legal aid bill is around 50 per cent more than the entire budget of the Crown Office and, since the 2008 banking crash, has relieved tax-payers of over £1 billion. Many solicitors' legal aid lust has been exposed. Kilmarnock court lawyer Niels Lockhart raked in £600,000 of 'excessive and unnecessary' claims, only to receive a slap on the wrist, and Glasgow solic-itor Steven Anderson was able to claim £560,330 in a single year.

Still nothing is done about taxpayers paying the bills of wealthy criminals like Barry Hughes and Michael Voudouri. Mr and Mrs Hughes racked up a £176,000 legal aid bill before their £50,000 Dubai holiday, while VAT fraudster Voudouri stole millions from taxpayers who then met his £769,000 bill. Placard-waving legal aid briefs have actually staged public demos demanding ever more loot. Their poverty pleas are as genuine as the stories they have to mouth for criminal clients.

If politicians were sincere about universal access to jus-tice, they would scrap legal aid and replace it with a net-work of public defenders. The genuinely impoverished would get representation while legal aid bottom-feeders – ripped from the teat of public subsidy – would learn to live on market rates, just like the rest of us.

One of the problems about working as a journalist is daily exposure to lawyers. Every news story is subjected to legal scrutiny, and I experienced occasions where lawyers were pressured through back channels to soften or even spike damaging tales about their brethren, cronies or clients.

Some newspaper lawyers came to enjoy and abuse the power and influence of being a man on the inside. Paul McBride QC topped up his generous income with shifts at the *Daily Record*, *Sunday Mail* and then *The Scottish Sun* – but certainly not for modest payments. McBride's reputation as a Mr Fixit extended beyond the Crown. Using mostly charm but occasionally menace, he could also pull strings with the press. At the *Sunday Mail* I wrote a story about a businessman friend of gangster Jamie 'The Iceman' Stevenson. When McBride came in, he already knew about my story and came straight over to demand a printed copy, something he had never done before. With his feet on the desk, he took a red pen through the mention of the businessman's child abuse conviction. I had been tipped off that he might try something like this. McBride initially tried to claim it was because the conviction was 'spent', but when I pointed out that that argument was groundless, he deployed persuasion to get his way. He suggested that we could come to an understanding where the conviction would be deleted and, in exchange, I would be given other stories. Absolutely no way, I replied.

McBride then tried to play down the seriousness of the conviction. He admitted knowing this because he had defended the businessman in the abuse case! This glaring conflict of interest should have forced him to back off, but McBride was bombproof, legal royalty, pals with the big bosses, had friends in high places and was used to getting his own way.

Unable to stay silent, I made my feelings clear in an email to my editor. I wrote:

McBride made various attempts to justify this censorship because the 'spent' conviction laws do not apply.

Given that his legal reason was bogus, McBride attempted to distort the facts and began a charm offensive. McBride said that the conviction was not serious and that —— was only a child at the time. I pointed out that —— plead guilty to committing the abuse between the ages of 12 and 15. McBride then suggested that what —— did was standard 'behind the bike sheds' behaviour. This is offensive and wrong.

—— admitted abusing three children (two girls and a boy) over a two-year period. One female victim was seven when it started. The eldest was 10. They were all in care.

For good measure, I pointed out that before McBride's meddling, the most cautious lawyer on our payroll had already okayed the story and that the conviction featured in a book written by a *Sunday Mail* colleague.

I added, 'We're well used to corrupt legal advice and old pals' acts, but Saturday's experience plumbed new depths. It is harder exposing these people when contacts have no faith in the paper's ability to tell a simple truth.'

I did not receive a reply. The seething editor's only issue was why I had contaminated his inbox with this hazardous email. This was the last occasion I received 'advice' from McBride, who died in Pakistan five weeks later.

19

THE UNTOUCHABLES

Ever since William Beck was convicted of robbery 36 years ago, he has waged a passionate and dogged campaign to prove his innocence.

He was 20 when the police arrested him for alleged assault in Whitburn, West Lothian. At the police station he was identified as one of two axe-wielding men responsible for another crime – the robbery of a Post Office van in nearby Livingston. It was impossible, he remonstrated, as he was at home in Glasgow on that day. The CID men, having heard it all before, told Beck to save it for the judge. The judge, Lord Dunpark, jailed him for six years.

The police and Crown Office case stank. Two witnesses, including an off-duty police officer, identified Beck as the robbery driver. However, a note made by Beck's lawyer on the day of his identification said the officer did so 'without even looking down the parade'. There were other holes and inconsistencies surrounding the credibility of ID evidence and information withheld from the defence. While prisons are full of those shouting about their innocence, few keep doing so after almost four decades.

When he finally won a right to appeal, he did not get justice – not even close. When his day at the appeal court arrived in 2006, he was crestfallen when three judges rejected his argument against an earlier decision not to allow a time extension. It was not until seven years later that he made a stupefying discovery. One of the three judges that day in 2006 had been Lord Johnston – who was the son of Lord Dunpark, the judge who had put him in prison. Even worse, the judge in charge of the 2006 hearing was Lord Osborne, aka Kenneth Osborne. He had been the Crown's advocate depute who prosecuted Beck in 1982. The only thing more shocking would have been if the third judge had been hiding a past career as a 1980s CID officer in West Lothian but he, at least, had no known links to the original trial.

Beck explained all of this to me, saying, 'There are supposedly rules in place to ensure judges don't get involved in cases where they have some kind of conflict. It's clear to me that he should have declared his connection and stepped aside.' I raised a quizzical eyebrow and wondered whether Beck's claims could be true. He was spot on.

After putting it to Lord Osborne, the only survivor of the trio, he told me, 'You'll appreciate that an advocate depute prosecutes a great many cases and I have no recollection of this one. If it had been drawn to my attention that I had any involvement as a prosecutor, I would have recused myself but I had no recollection of it.'

Beck attempted to raise his concerns about the two judges. Down came the legal shutters on this noisy nuisance from Glasgow. It was bad enough that he had been denied legal aid throughout the process. One wonders where the placard-waving legal aid guardians and their universal justice ethos were when they were needed.

When Beck finally returned to court to raise the unfairness of what had gone before, the judge only responded to his legal aid gripe but did not address the issue of judicial conflict tainting the process. Beck went on to tell a Holyrood committee, 'How can they ignore it completely, I hear everyone ask? Simply because they can. This proves that not only did two judges sit on my appeal when they ought not to have done so, but there has been a concerted attempt from the judiciary to cover this up since.'

Beck – still determined to clear his name – may agree with journalist and author Rod Liddle who, in his book *Selfish, Whining Monkeys*, writes:

> Should we kill all the lawyers, do you suppose? There are still some people around who disagree with this notion, considering it 'too extreme' and 'an overreaction' and 'illegal'. Of course this last objection somewhat loses its force if we killed all the judges, too – and indeed it is probably the judges with whom I would start, if I had to organise the whole thing.

Liddle, while clearly joking, may have a point. History tells us how Scotland's judges accrued great power and wealth without the burden of accountability or transparency. A self-styled judicial 'aristocracy' bloomed following the 1707 Act of Union which shut down Scotland's parliament and created a power vacuum in Edinburgh. The judges, led by the Lord President, staged a land-grab to occupy the politicians' vacant Parliament House and became the voice of authority in Scotland as she was ruled from London for three centuries. The vast majority of senior judges are still old, white men. It was not until 1996 that a woman joined their club.

No one could sensibly argue against an independent judiciary as a vital bulwark against meddling politicians, but small reforms take centuries and are opposed at every turn with shrieks of 'judicial independence'. Over the years I have written about judges who have committed benefit fraud, had sex with prostitutes, inflicted domestic violence and driven while drunk. There is a long roll call of sheriffs whose arrogant conduct on the bench is amusing and staggering in equal measure. They are the scowling tyrants who wield dictatorial power in 'their' courts, issue bizarre and erratic pronouncements, glory in prejudice, treat decent people with antipathy and demonstrate ignorance of the laws they are supposed to administer.

It is telling that more effective than any politician or journalist has been legal blogger Peter Cherbi – smeared following the Les Cumming stabbing (see p. 138) – whose reasoned arguments led to a public register of judicial recusals. Cherbi's campaign for a register of interests causes judges to splutter with indignation, but its simple and persuasive logic has won backing from cross-party MSPs, law academics, the media and civil servants who oversee judicial complaints. The previous Lord President, Lord Gill, twice snubbed a Holyrood invitation to discuss Cherbi's proposal. He cited the Scotland Act, which protects judges from being forced to explain their courtroom decisions but does not exempt them from discussing how the judiciary operates. Gill's decision to then give a speech about judicial ethics in Qatar, a financier of global Islamist terror groups, where human rights are virtually non-existent, was viewed by some as contempt.

The power in the hands of Scotland's judges is amplified by their aggressive opposition to transparency and curled-lip contempt for accountability. Courteous conduct, effective discipline, open and fair appointments, common sense, and consistency in sentencing and declaring hidden financial and business interests still seem a long way off. The judiciary seems to think it is still the 18th century.

The core values of secrecy and an aloof disdain towards the hoi polloi also permeate the other branch of the legal elite, the Crown Office, led by the Lord Advocate – currently James Wolffe QC who, one day, is most likely also to become a judge. The Crown's main task is pretty simple – put suspects on trial, fairly and in a timely fashion, and prove their guilt. This should be done in the interest of the public, not that of the legal profession. Behind a thin veneer of competence, Scotland's prosecuting authority is borderline dysfunctional – in a perpetual state of chaos, pinballing from one disaster to the next and more interested in spinning tall tales to the public than serving it.

In 1996 12-year-old John Rogers was murdered in Lanarkshire. His alleged killer confessed on tape to police, but the evidence was inadmissible because of his mental state. The Crown proceeded regardless, the case collapsed and the suspect walked free. Two decades of suffering later, John's mother, Linda McConville, told me, 'The Crown should have seen the legal problem and should have held back because of it. It seems to be a case of "Thank you very much for your son's life but you can go home now" – even though they messed the case up.' Despite her anguish, no meaningful explanation or apology was ever proffered. The show moved on and she was left behind with her treasured photos.

Another scandal I investigated involved nine police officers being hospitalised during a Wild West-style pub riot in Glasgow on the day of an Old Firm match. Two suspects – a Glasgow gangster and his son – walked free after four years of churn culminated with the discovery of fatally botched paperwork. One of the female police victims, whose neck was almost snapped and who resigned in disgust, said to me, 'I saw straightforward cases being

flung out, with a red pen being put through them by
the Crown.'

Another farce I reported was the prosecution of nine
alleged members of the Daniel mob who faced 25 charges.
There were 750 items of evidence, 270 witnesses and nine
sets of lawyers – solicitors and senior counsel for each suspect – who raked in handsome sums of legal aid. Yet, at
the latest possible moment, the Crown announced a deal
which resulted in *one* suspect admitting a *single* charge of
drug-dealing. The rest walked out, all innocent, to the
despair of police officers. The judge, Lord Turnbull, a former Crown prosecutor, said, 'Some observers may wonder
why it is in the public interest to bring these proceedings
for them to be then comprehensively abandoned today.'

The culture of delays or churn is not just a defence ruse
– it is often caused by Crown inefficiency. Sit in a sheriff
court any day and, like toppling dominoes, case after case
is put off, adjourned, declared not ready or kicked into the
long grass. In some jurisdictions, the issue of plea deals are
up front and visible. While it may be unpalatable to allow
a suspect to admit some charges in exchange for others
being dropped or softened, it saves court time and money,
and spares witnesses the ordeal of testifying. In Scotland,
this controversial tactic was sneaked in through the back
door. Details of such deals are never publicised and it is
up to the press to decipher whenever grubby agreements
have been reached in this shadow process. This is made
more difficult because court-based press agencies, part of
the apparatus and reliant upon it, rarely report such deals
or, if they do, couch them in flowery euphemisms. With no
public or political debate, Crown prosecutors also quietly
accept the use of 'supergrass' witnesses to secure convictions. As with plea deals, these cases can be just as repugnant, with public ignorance seemingly a matter of policy.

One unsettling investigation I conducted in 2010 featured a plea deal and supergrass cocktail. Heroin dealer Gary Edmonds admitted luring murder victim Paul Boland to a rendezvous with his killer in Clydebank. Edmonds, who also watched the murder take place and helped dispose of the killer's bloodstained BMW, was charged over his involvement. He then later agreed to turn grass in exchange for his charges to be dropped. In another tawdry twist, the killer, John Mullen, then struck a side deal with the Crown, admitting guilt in exchange for a murder charge against his own son being binned. It wasn't justice being seen to be done – it was a secretive carve-up.

All these cases and countless others prompt the usual howls from MSPs demanding an explanation. Presumably MSPs' letters are filed in the recycling bin because no proper justification is ever forthcoming. Whenever politicians, the press or public seek answers in relation to the latest Crown fiasco, they hear the white noise of 'after full and careful consideration of the facts and circumstances . . . blah, blah, blah'.

Perhaps after less than two decades in existence, Holyrood still lacks the maturity and confidence to realise that its members are in charge, on behalf of us, the public. While MSPs remain neutered or awestruck by the law, the Crown and judiciary will never prioritise the rights of victims and witnesses, embrace transparency, explain why cases are dropped and when deals are done, end churn and, frankly, explain when things go wrong.

20

DANGER: OLD FIRM

Which of the two incidents was more absurd? Was it the Loyalist terrorist and multiple killer Michael Stone fixing me with his best death-stare and growling, 'You look like a Catholic?' or perhaps an Alsatian dog called Souness baring his white fangs and emitting a deep growl for my daring to ask for his 'Celtic paw'?

Stone was jailed for 638 years in 1988 for attacking an IRA funeral in Belfast using hand grenades and pistols, killing three mourners and wounding scores more. He was one of hundreds of terrorists released due to the Good Friday Agreement. Just months later, in November 2000, he visited Glasgow to attend an Old Firm match. Realising that we had got wind of his stay at the city's Hilton Hotel and were lurking in the lobby, he called an impromptu press conference which he interspersed with snide speculation about my religion, his face feet away from mine. I didn't respond to Stone's menace.

Souness, named after former Rangers manager Graeme Souness, was an imposing beast owned by Liz McDonald, the estranged mother of actor Robert Carlyle. On her living room wall was a large framed photo of Souness – the dog, of course – wearing an Orange Order sash. When asked to give his 'Rangers paw' he obliged. It was only a request for his left 'Celtic paw' that prompted snarling defiance.

Growling Stone and growling Souness were amusing, weird and disturbing in their own ways, and help illustrate how the tribalism of Rangers versus Celtic, Protestant versus Catholic, continues to pervade life in some parts of Scotland. One thing you learn as a journalist in Glasgow is that the Old Firm sells newspapers more than any other subject – even crime and sex – but that to provoke the two clubs is to play with fire as two of my editors found out by paying with their jobs.

According to some Rangers fans I didn't work for the *Sunday Mail* but the *Sunday Liam*, while some Celtic rivals branded it the *Sunday Mason*. Similarly, the *Daily Record* was the *Daily Ranger* or *Daily Rebel*. Partick Thistle fan, you say? Aye, right. So who do you *really* support? You cannot win.

An early Old Firm scrape saw me dispatched to Celtic Park, where Hollywood actor Robert Duvall was attending the 1998 Scottish Cup Final between Rangers and Hearts. Spotting the star's shiny bald head in a swarm of people, I persuaded him to stop for a quick photo while Steve McNeil, a Rangers-supporting photographer, grabbed a scarf from a random fan. As Steve's camera was clicking, neither of us noticed that emblazoned on the held-aloft scarf was the political and religious demand to 'KEEP ULSTER PROTESTANT', which prompted a minor storm. Duvall went on to produce *A Shot at Glory*, an odd movie charting the giant-killing cup run of fictional Kilnockie FC, whose top striker was, for some reason, played by Ally McCoist. Responding to the scarf row, innocent abroad Duvall later explained, 'It was just something somebody handed to me and I got my picture taken. But that's really what I'm here for. To learn more about soccer and the people who are involved in it.'

The following year I embarked on an Old Firm adventure worthy of Belgian cartoon journalist Tintin. Having saved Celtic from oblivion, Fergus McCann had quit the club and vanished from Scotland, and my boss was desperate to track him down. When a contact confidently provided me with an address for McCann in the French coastal village of Arès, near Bordeaux, I was sent straight to the airport. Accompanied by photographer Gaetan Cotton, fizzing with excitement at the thought of French wine on expenses, we found what we hoped was the McCann residence – a large house hidden behind a high metal fence and imposing gate. As hours dragged by, trapped in a sun-baked car, there was no sign of the brusque little businessman famous for his mid-Atlantic accent and trademark bunnet.

Having almost given up hope, the gates of the mansion swung open and out he stepped. Gaetan got snap-happy as McCann, without his bunnet, beetled along in a head-turning ensemble of bright red Bermuda shorts, matching knee-high socks and canary-yellow shirt. At Chez Alcide brasserie, the chic natives stopped talking to stare and chuckle in bemusement at 'ze very funny little man' marching past them in the midday sun.

Job done, we made the bonus discovery that McCann's family home happened to be beside a statue carved with flying saucers and a Latin welcome message for any visitors from outer space who happened to drop in on Earth. The story signed off with: 'It's not known when the McCanns will say au revoir to France before heading to their new home in Bermuda. Before they go, perhaps someone should tell the folk of Arès a little green man has already paid a visit.'

Just prior to our French adventure, a video had emerged of Rangers vice-chairman Donald Findlay QC performing 'The Sash', a song regarded by many as sectarian and anti-Catholic, which forced his resignation.

A few weeks later, my boss told me that the *Sunday Mail* had a photo of John Greig, Rangers PR boss and legendary ex-captain, miming the playing of a flute with a bottle, which had been taken in Canada at a supporters' club event where sectarian anthems were sung. It was Saturday afternoon and I was sent to Tynecastle, where Rangers were playing Hearts, with an instruction to ask Greig about it as he boarded the team bus. Jostling with autograph-hunting fans, I thrust out the picture and tape recorder and sought an explanation from the man just voted 'Greatest Ever Ranger'.

He told me, 'I don't even remember that picture being taken. It's ancient history. I was only larking about with the boys. Are you going to put that in the paper? Remember, you've got to come back and work with us.'

Little did I know that I was a mere pawn in what would become a battle royal between Rangers chairman David Murray and *Sunday Mail* editor Jim Cassidy. There could be only one winner. The edited version of the story included the following:

> Greig's 'performance' is sure to anger Rangers supremo David Murray, who has attempted to stamp out bigotry at the club.
>
> He [Greig] is the latest to join the growing band of those who have disgraced Rangers. Now John Greig – the man known simply as 'The Legend' – joins the Ibrox Hall of Shame.

This additional editorialising was off the mark. Murray was not angry with Greig but furious with Cassidy.

In an unprecedented attack, Murray shot back:

> After reading the front page article of the *Sunday Mail*, one has to question the motivation and integrity of an editor [Cassidy] wishing to print such a story regarding one of the most respected and popular men in Scottish football.
>
> One must question the objective and, in my opinion, this seems to be an effort to destroy not only the good reputation of a decorated Scottish footballing legend, but also to continue to tarnish the reputation of Rangers Football Club.

While the story clearly stated that the photo was nine years old, Greig's backers argued that its age made it irrelevant and its publication a cheap smear.

The Greig picture exposed interesting differences of opinion in the press. *The Herald* newspaper, friendly to Murray, sniffily dismissed it with 69 words tucked away on page two, while columnist Bill Leckie of *The Scottish Sun* wrote:

> He [Greig] will, of course, remind us that the offending picture of him was taken nine years ago. I would remind HIM that 1990 was a year after they were supposed to have seen the light by signing the semi-Catholic Mo Johnston.
>
> And anyway, it's not as if he was naive to the ways of the bigot nine years ago. He's been a Ranger to his socks for 42 years, captained them for 15, managed them for five, spin-doctored them for 10. He knows EXACTLY what it means when he goes to an official function and joins in the Fenian-baiting.

What angers me is the chairman's rabble-rous-
ing insistence that it's those who highlight incidents such as these who cause the problem, not
those involved in them. David Murray should be
bigger and brighter than that.

Murray flexed his financial muscles by withdrawing
Daily Record billboards and removing the names of both
papers from ball-boys' shirts at the next home match. The
parent Trinity Mirror board in London knew that if the
Greig affair escalated into a club-orchestrated boycott by
Rangers fans and the withdrawal of access to Ibrox for its
journalists, it would be devastating. The board did not
share Leckie's punchy defence and, a month later, Cassidy
was evicted from the editor's chair.

Greig's comment, 'Remember you've got to come back
and work with us,' was seen by some as evidence that
Cassidy's axing owed more to pacifying Rangers, protecting the company's bottom line and maintaining an
incestuous business relationship than any moral outrage.

The newspaper group had acquired the publishing
rights to the club's official magazine, which was part of
an estimated £1 million of annual, two-way transactions
between them and Rangers. This was an obvious conflict of interest. How could their editors independently
publish stories about a football club with whom they had
vested business interests?

Cassidy was replaced by pugnacious Fleet Street veteran
Peter Cox, who then went on to become *Daily Record* editor. He lasted three years there before he too was forced
out – one of the reasons being that he upset Celtic. Cox
ran an infamous front-page headline 'THUGS AND
THIEVES' over a story about an alleged fracas between a
Record photographer and some Celtic players on their 2002

Christmas night out in Newcastle. This caused a boycott of the paper by some Celtic supporters, who also lobbied for Trinity Mirror's publishing of the club's official magazine to be cancelled, which all sounds rather familiar – as does the ending. Cox clung on for a few months before he was sacked, to be replaced by Bruce Waddell, a good chum of Murray who now works in PR.

During this time, Murray was treated as a living deity, worshipped by the Ibrox legions and idolised by some sports, news and business journalists – grown men spellbound by bombast and boasts such as vowing to spend £10 for every £5 spent by Celtic. This was the era in which Murray was willing to allow Rangers to lose a chunk of sponsorship income from the *Daily Record* and *Sunday Mail* in order to make a point – to show who was boss after the Greig affair.

Armchair business gurus now nod their heads knowingly and explain that actually it had been perfectly obvious to them all along that Rangers was built on a mountain of Murray Group bank debt which would be called in one day. When the hubristic house of cards came crashing down, Murray was forced to meekly surrender debt-crippled Rangers to Craig Whyte for a one-pound coin, and the rest is history.

But while Murray was at the peak of his power, it was no easy task for journalists to take on the dark subject of the Old Firm and bigotry. My eyes glaze over and my ears became deaf at the Old Firm wall of noise that screams from sports pages and broadcasts. How can so many millions of words have been spent debating the tedious minutiae of two football clubs? Even worse than the obsession is the bigotry and hate. I have wondered if Rangers and Celtic are actually a single business that dreamt up a genius marketing wheeze of religious division to grow rich.

From a young age, I learned to despise the twisted glorification of terrorism. Home-grown fans shouting about the IRA or UVF at a football match in Scotland are shameful and cowardly. They never risked a sniper's bullet or a car bomb. These morons should hop on a ferry to Northern Ireland, where they could try serenading the countless families whose loved ones have died at the hands of terrorists.

Six years after Cassidy's sacking, BBC *Panorama* produced *Scotland's Secret Shame,* which examined the ingrained nature of sectarianism and violence that blights the Old Firm and its fixtures. Unlike the press, the BBC could not be so easily nobbled by schmoozing or boycott threats.

Murray, ever the showman, responded by flourishing a 10-point plan which Rangers fans must adhere to. One was to wear only 'traditional team colours', which was a reference to the club's earlier production of an orange shirt, explained as a tribute to their Dutch players but widely seen as a nod towards the Protestant organisation the Orange Order. A few months after Murray's blueprint to beat the bigots, I wandered past a Rangers shop in Glasgow and noticed something remarkable about the brand-new items on display. The shelves and racks were laden with an abundance of newly arrived orange-coloured lines – shirts, baseball caps, even cute little gifts for babies.

Another of the 10 points was to 'monitor the sale and advertising of retail products to ensure nothing offensive or reasonably perceived as offensive reaches the public'. Had Murray's 10-point plan not reached the club's own retail department? Or, as a journalist might cynically suspect, perhaps it had just been a knee-jerk PR exercise? When I phoned a club PR representative for comment, they frostily informed me that someone would talk to the editor about it. Going over a journalist's head is common,

but it is a most counter-productive PR tactic as it only gal-
vanises the determination to get the story out.

A handful of sports journalists, people like Bill Leckie,
Graham Spiers, Gerry McNee and others, should be
commended for challenging the deep-rooted poison of
religious hatred amongst some Rangers and Celtic fans, at
a time when even talking about it was taboo.

Eight years after the Greig affair, when the issue of sectarianism had gone mainstream and was finally of interest
to politicians and the football authorities, McNee wrote in
the *News of the World*:

> Now, as they [Rangers and Celtic] come under
> massive pressure from domestic and interna-
> tional football governing bodies, the clubs don't
> want these people whose money they took and to
> whom they turned a blind eye when the threat
> wasn't there. Do they honestly believe they can
> just flick a switch and be rid of them?
>
> Sectarianism is like the foot-and-mouth virus.
> You can't cut bits out. It has to be eradicated. All
> the causes must be culled – the music, flags, ban-
> ners, songs and chants.

A strange and sinister episode that took place inside
Ibrox stadium in 1999 came to my attention in 2004. As far
as the official record is concerned, a man called William
Taube died after falling down stairs during a function at
the stadium's Edmiston suite. Five years later, a witness
approached me with some startling claims. Not only was
Taube a member of the proscribed Loyalist UVF terror
group, but the 'Blue Mist' function he attended was a
fundraiser with ex-UVF prisoners among the guests. The
witness, a bouncer on duty that night, provided a different

take to the official version. According to him, Taube had been in a fight with another man which resulted in him falling down stairs and smashing his head. The witness claimed that Taube's friends then gave chase down the street to the other man, whose fate was unknown. Finally, he alleged that police officers had threatened him by saying if he didn't keep his mouth shut they would tell Taube's UVF pals that he was delaying the release of the body.

Scotland has a blind spot with cases of sudden and unexplained deaths. Had Taube died in England, the circumstances would have been subject of a public inquest conducted by a coroner. In Scotland, the equivalent of a fatal accident enquiry only happens at the behest of the Crown Office. For Taube, there was no fatal accident enquiry and no post mortem. The police had not even informed the public about his sudden death. It was as if it had never happened. Not a single word about it was reported until the witness decided to break his silence half a decade later.

I tracked down Taube's mother and carefully relayed the witness's detailed claims through her partially opened front door. To my great surprise, she was not in the least surprised, telling me, 'I said there was a cover-up at the time and still believe it. William's death wasn't an accident. I even fell out with the police and told one in particular he was telling us a pack of lies – he seemed determined to get it out of the way quickly. I went to the procurator fiscal's office several months after William's death and the woman couldn't get me out of there quick enough. I insisted on a post mortem but the fiscal said it was only a head injury and that was all there was to it.'

Suddenly a male relative appeared behind her and abruptly ended our conversation with a slammed door and shouted threats. I was firmly told not to come back. To this day, no proper explanation from the authorities has been forthcoming.

Perhaps the official version suited everyone – Rangers, the UVF, the police, the family and politicians of all shades who were fighting to sell the distasteful elements of the fledgling Good Friday Agreement – signed a year earlier – especially the mass release of murderous monsters like Stone and his Republican equivalents.

21

THE WINDOW CLEANER

On a quietly ordinary Sunday morning I was awoken by a window cleaner at my front door.

Pale-faced and unsteady on his feet, he supported his slight frame against the red sandstone wall and politely requested a glass of water. While on his rounds he had become unwell and could not continue. I fetched water from the kitchen and returned to the door. His speech was quiet, stilted and breathy. His demeanour was sheepish and awkward, bordering on the servile. He had another favour to ask. Could I possibly lend him £20? This would allow him to go home and rest rather than stay out working, which he was clearly unfit to do.

I had no reason to doubt what he said, so handed £20 to the wiry, grey-haired little man who expressed immense gratitude. With his thanks came a promise to clean my windows the following day when he was better. The £20 would be an upfront payment for two return visits. He did not come back the next day or at all.

Weeks later I saw him in the distance but he skulked around a corner and took off. A few weeks after that he was back in my street, perched precariously on a first-floor tenement window-ledge, he being a window cleaner with no ladders. I shouted up, 'You never came back to clean

my windows. Where's my twenty pounds?' He replied,
'I've no' got it,' with an unexpected note of defiance in
his voice. I told him to give me whatever payment he was
about to get for the job being done, but he did not like this
suggestion and angrily demanded me to leave him alone.
The brief stand-off ended when a middle-aged woman
appeared at the window and cast a look which told me to
stop harassing her window-cleaner. Causing him to fall to
his death seemed like an overreaction about £20, so I left
empty handed, muttering a few insults as I went.

I would later learn this was no ordinary window cleaner.
He did not need a glass of water from me or my £20.
His claim of illness was a well-polished act of deception.
Falling to his death would have been too good for him.
The epiphany came two years later as, off on holiday, I
eased into the seat of a plane and picked up a copy of the
Daily Record. The front-page headline was 'ODD-JOB MAN
IS A RAPIST' with the sub-heading, 'Sex beast unmasked
in hunt for Angelika'.

Angelika Kluk was a 23-year-old Polish woman studying in Glasgow who was missing, feared dead. The story
began: 'The odd-job man wanted over the disappearance
of Polish student Angelika Kluk is a convicted child rapist. The man who called himself Pat McLaughlin is really
named Peter Tobin.' As I looked at the grainy photo of
the odd-job man wanted by police, it was one of those
moments when a face is familiar but the crucial details
of who, when and where remain just out of reach of your
memory. Then the penny dropped. Tobin was my window cleaner. The jolt of realisation was almost physical
in its force and my mind began to race. When he came
to my door that Sunday morning, I was 31 and living
with my girlfriend. What could have happened had I not
been there when he came calling? Was Tobin hoping to

find my girlfriend home alone and, if so, what was his intent?

The thoughts of what might have been were chilling, and that was before the discovery that Tobin was not only a rapist but a serial killer, convicted of three murders and suspected of many more. His first known victim was 15-year-old Vicky Hamilton, from Bathgate, West Lothian, who was last seen in February 1991. The second was Dinah McNicol, aged 18, of Tillingham in Essex, who disappeared in August 1991.

Two years later, Tobin attacked two 14-year-old girls at his flat in Havant, Hampshire. Holding them at knifepoint, he forced them to drink alcohol, stabbed one and raped them, all while his six-year-old son was at home. He fled with his son and left the gas on with the intent that an explosion would hide his tracks, but one of the girls awoke and raised the alarm. For this atrocity, Tobin was jailed for 14 years but was out after 10 and crept back to Paisley, the home town of William 'Basil' Burns. What is it about malevolent creeps from that town coming to my front door?

Itinerant Tobin worked as a handyman and used up to 40 aliases during a life spent preying on young women while drifting around central Scotland and southern England. The discovery that he routinely feigned illness made perfect sense, as I had seen his accomplished play-acting first hand.

Tobin's reign of horror ended in September 2006 with the rape and murder of Kluk, whose body was hidden beneath the floor of a Catholic church in Glasgow's Anderston district, less than two miles from my own home. It was his first of three convictions for murder.

Once convicted, almost immediately the question began to be asked of Tobin: was he the notorious Bible John? Over a 20-month period in the late 1960s, three women were killed after nights out at Glasgow's Barrowland Ballroom. The first was Patricia Docker, 25, who was found strangled in February 1968. The following August, 32-year-old mother of three Jemima McDonald was found dead, having being strangled with her own stockings. Finally, Helen Puttock, 29, was raped, then strangled with her tights in October 1969. Helen had been out with her sister Jean and they had shared a taxi home with a polite and well-spoken man who said his name was John. During the journey, the man quoted from the Bible, spawning the nickname which generated countless headlines and gripped the public, whose fascination remains undimmed almost half a century later.

Slurring, saloon-bar detectives perched on stools in dingy dives will tell anyone daft enough to listen that that they *know* who Bible John really was. Buy them a pint and they'll tell you: my neighbour's postman's uncle's butcher . . . that kind of thing. Whether the killer even quoted from the Bible or simply referred to it is subject to dispute as, like so much of the saga, it is often hard to discern where facts blend into hearsay, assumption and legend.

Criminologist Professor David Wilson spent three years researching the unsolved murders for his 2010 book *The Lost British Serial Killer*, in which he concluded that Tobin was Bible John. In a press interview, Wilson said, 'I didn't set out to prove Tobin was Bible John, but I would stake my professional reputation on it.'

I was intrigued by the increasing body of evidence and opinion which supported this theory. Tobin had moved away from Glasgow in late 1969, the year of the final murder, after marrying his first wife, whom he met at the Barrowland. Tobin was known to be driven to violence by the menstrual cycle, and all three of Bible John's victims were menstruating at the time they were murdered. In addition, Tobin purports to have Catholic beliefs.

I spent hours leafing through hundreds of yellowing, musty and fragile press cuttings from the time of the murders as well as modern, digitised archives. Something was missing from this vast reservoir of claims, counterclaims and conspiracy theories. Not once over 41 years could I find evidence of any journalist haven spoken with Helen's sister Jean. The press cuttings could not even agree on what her surname was.

Having been dropped off by her sister and the killer, Jean was the only surviving witness to have seen Bible John, as the taxi driver was long dead. It was her recollection of the shared journey with Bible John which provided detectives with everything they knew about him and generated Scotland's first police photofit, which bears an uncanny similarity to a young Tobin. If anyone could come close to answering whether Tobin was Bible John, it was Jean. The unsettling memory of Tobin as my window cleaner fuelled my determination to find out. I decided to track down Jean, which was easier said than done – not least due to her having had four surnames in her life, the first being Gowans when she was born in 1936.

Once I established her name was now Jean McLachlan, I set about trying to find her, but that too was not as straightforward as one would expect. David Wilson had no leads, having been told by the police that she may have emigrated to New Zealand. I finally tracked down a relative who said that Jean was living in Ayrshire, but I had run out of time to make the trip for that week's edition as it was late on a Friday afternoon. The relative explained that Jean was very unwell but that I could get in touch the following week to see if she might speak to me, to answer that one big question about Tobin.

As it turned out, next week was too late. I never got to ask Jean the question as she died of cancer just two days later on Sunday, 12 September 2010, at the age of 74, taking her answer to the grave. It may have been that even if I had reached her sooner, she would have been reluctant to conjure up ghosts from the past.

During my research I had come across Jean's son, who had plenty to say about Bible John and the police investigation led by detective Joe Beattie. Sitting in his flat in Maryhill less than two weeks after his mum's death, he dropped what appeared to be a bombshell revelation. Asked if Jean had ever suggested that Tobin was the man in the taxi that fateful night, he said, 'She told me that it was Tobin a fortnight ago today, which was five days before she died. She said that's him. She was a hundred-per-cent sure he was the man in the taxi with her sister. I asked her – I said, "Is it Tobin?" She said, "Yes, it was him." I hate Tobin for what he's put my family through. I even wanted to get arrested so that I could go to [HMP] Saughton and do him in.'

Unfortunately, like so much else to do with Bible John, Jean's son's extraordinary and unequivocal admission was not as clear and simple as it first appeared. He was highly emotional and his story became tangled in contradictions and repetition as he segued from burning rage to tortured pain and back again. I sought out other family members to see if they could corroborate his claims, but they cautioned me against taking what he said at face value. Like so many journalists, I had set out to establish hard facts about Bible John, only to be led into a hall of mirrors where nothing was quite as it seemed.

The resulting story, headlined 'BIBLE JOHN: THE END', told how Jean's death meant that any slim chance of a successful prosecution had died with her. I contacted victim Helen Puttock's husband, George who said, 'Now Jean has gone and more time passes, it will never be solved. Jeanie always swore that she would never forget the face of Helen's killer and I believed her.'

The only other person left who can answer the question is obviously Tobin himself. But such grotesque monsters usually enjoy the power of holding on to the darkest secrets about their crimes which they then use to taunt and torment families who have suffered more than can be imagined.

Tobin will fester in prison until the day he dies, as will Angus Sinclair, another serial killer who got away with murder for far too long and who refuses to disclose details of his crimes.

Sinclair has been convicted of killing four women, but the true number is suspected of being six, possibly more. He was 16 when he killed for the first time. Catherine Reehill, a seven-year-old neighbour in Glasgow, was lured away, raped and strangled. For reasons best known to the judge, Sinclair was sentenced to 10 years in prison, serving only six, despite a psychiatrist's report prepared after the 1961 murder warning: 'I do not think that any form of psychotherapy is likely to benefit his condition and he will constitute a danger from now onwards. He is obsessed by sex, and given the minimum of opportunity, he will repeat these offences.'

And repeat them he did. In 1977 he was thought to have murdered six women in a seven-month period, followed by another in 1978. The 1977 victims were Frances Barker, 37; Hilda McAuley, 36; Agnes Cooney, 23; and Anna Kenny, 20, all from Glasgow, as well as Christine Eadie and Helen Scott, both 17, from Edinburgh. The next year he sexually assaulted and murdered 17-year-old Mary Gallacher in Glasgow.

In 1982 he was convicted and jailed for rape and sexual attacks against 11 children aged six to 14. It was not until 2000 that a review of the Gallacher case resulted in his conviction for her murder the following year. Then, in 2014, he was convicted of killing Eadie and Scott, in what is known as the World's End murders (after the pub of that name in which the girls had been drinking on the night of their murder). This conviction for double murder confirmed his status as a serial killer amidst much crowing and backslapping by police and prosecutors, but they had absolutely nothing to be proud of.

Not only had Scotland's worst serial killer got away with it for far too long, causing immeasurable devastation to countless people, but an initial World's End prosecution in 2007 had been botched, resulting in Sinclair's farcical acquittal. The only good thing to come out of that debacle was a change in the law giving the Crown the right to prosecute someone for a crime of which they have already been acquitted. Neatly, Sinclair was the first to feel the effects of double jeopardy, which enabled his 2014 retrial.

When I took a phone call from a long-standing and trusted contact just after Sinclair's eventual World's End conviction, what he told me made my blood run cold. Peter McLeod was a bright, honest and capable detective in an era when those traits often seemed less important than being in with the right people and when playing fast and loose with evidence was commonplace. McLeod is the kind of man who will stand up and be counted – who will speak out over an injustice, no matter how difficult that might be.

In 2001 he was working in the Strathclyde Police Force Intelligence Bureau, and Sinclair was yet to stand trial for the Gallacher murder. McLeod had pored over reams of intelligence from a series of unsolved murders in the

Strathclyde Police area. On the basis of his painstaking analysis, he then wrote and submitted an internal memo in which Sinclair was named for the first time as the suspect in the murders of Kenny, McAuley and Cooney.

His memo, dated February 2001, urged senior officers to send the case to a specialist unit in England which analyses sex killings across the UK. But there was no appetite from above to accede to his request. Quite the opposite: there was a naked hostility towards the recommendation. One senior officer made it clear that McLeod should back down. Not long after that, McLeod left the intelligence unit and the following year learned that his memo had been buried and his suggestions ignored. Why would the police do this? Why would they aggressively shun an explosive memo, based on hard evidence and written by a trusted and respected detective which alleged that Sinclair was a serial killer? There could, in McLeod's eyes, be only one shocking conclusion, and that was a police cover-up.

A lorry driver called Thomas Young had already been found guilty of the 1977 killing of Frances Barker – a crime now widely accepted to have been committed by Sinclair. Young had served 37 years behind bars when he died in 2014, still protesting his innocence. McLeod delivered to me the following damning assessment: 'I think it's very likely that they [senior police officers] were aware that the conviction of Thomas Young was totally unsound. They couldn't risk it being looked at in detail because it would show up the fact that it was so similar to the others. They knew about Young and they were trying to put hurdles in the way. These people did everything they could to stop this being properly investigated.'

McLeod's memo had been too hot to handle. To probe deeper into the three other murders would only risk unwelcome scrutiny of the Young conviction – the kind of attention that trashes the reputation of police officers, possibly even putting them in jail. Even worse than the suspicion that Young was fitted up for murder were the extraordinary consequences of doing so. Barker had been the first of the six victims in the 1977 killing spree. The quick arrest and prosecution of Young would almost certainly have emboldened Sinclair.

Picture the scene – a shocked young Sinclair smiling gleefully at news reports of another man being swiftly dispatched to prison for a murder he had committed. If it is true that Sinclair did kill Barker – and there is no serious suggestion to the contrary – then the alleged police fit-up of Young could have served as a giant green light for Sinclair. As McLeod put it: 'By arresting Young, the police could have given Sinclair the confidence to keep on killing. They effectively gave him a licence to kill.'

In the face of some stiff competition, this story was perhaps the most shocking of any of the thousands I have written in almost 25 years. Yet not a single newspaper or broadcaster thought it worthy of attention, to the undoubted delight of Scotland's worst serial killer and relief of a few retired CID men.

22

'UNMASKED'

'UNMASKED' – like all the best headlines, needs no explaining, and journalists will never get tired of using it.

One of my first sorties into organised crime followed the murder of Tony McGovern, whose face appeared under the headline 'UNMASKED' alongside an account of his unlikely rich and famous friends and feud with Jamie 'The Iceman' Stevenson.

Linked directly with McGovern was the lawless world of gangster-run security firms which were on the brink of exploding into a decade of violence, corruption and abuse of public money – something akin to 1920s Chicago, according to one judge.

There was a constant supply of organised criminals who rose up more quickly than they could be unmasked – for every one exposed, two others appeared to take his place, like the Greek myth of the Hydra, a monstrous serpent which regenerates two new heads for each one chopped off.

In 2000 I unmasked Robert Wright and Les Brown, the drug-smugglers whose contacts included the Russian Mafia in Estonia and domestic drug-dealer Justin McAlroy, whose murder exposed murky connections between Labour and gangland.

That same year I exposed the drug-dealing Hamilton family of Stewarton, Ayrshire, who had links with outlawed terrorist groups the UVF and Red Hand Commandos. Their importation of Loyalist terror tactics into an ordinary Scottish community, targeting decent people with knives and guns, should have brought widespread outrage but, such is its fickle nature, most of the media paid no heed.

In 2003 it was the turn of north Glasgow crime gangs – the Daniels and Lyons – to be unmasked, although no one could have foreseen that their spat over stolen cocaine would evolve into Scotland's dirtiest and deadliest underworld war, which rages to this day.

Then Russell Stirton and his criminal fortune were dragged into the spotlight, which led me to his associate Barry Hughes. The unmasking of Hughes mutated into his PR game of distortedly presenting himself as celebrity rather than criminal.

In the same year, VAT fraudster Michael Voudouri, alongside his Edinburgh drug-dealing friend George 'Dode' Buchanan, came to my attention. Voudouri, who stole unknown millions of pounds from taxpayers, provided years of entertainment with his flamboyance. There was the outrageous spending of his loot on hiring celebrities for personal appearances and flying on private jets; there was his self-harming gloat on BBC's *Panorama* show about beating a Proceeds of Crime prosecution, and his dramatic flight from justice to northern Cyprus to, temporarily, avoid a prison sentence. That his family had publicly announced their intended flit on Facebook caused some embarrassment for the police and Crown Office. To Voudouri's spluttering astonishment, we tracked him down to his Cypriot lair by matching family Facebook photos of his distinctively shaped swimming pool to the satellite view of it on Google Maps. Not long after that, he swapped the Cypriot sunshine for a Scottish prison cell.

In 2005 I unmasked two key members of the Lyons gang, whose occupancy of Chirnsyde youth club was then still stubbornly supported by the police, the Labour Party and Glasgow City Council. We told how Steven Lyons and Ross Monaghan walked free from court on multiple night-club stabbing charges after witnesses refused to speak up. The cocky pair scarpered from the High Court in Glasgow to evade my photographer colleague. We gave chase but they got away – which we put right the next day by finding a hidden vantage point from which to capture their pho-tos. A decade would pass before I next set eyes on Lyons.

I then unmasked Annette Daniel and Jean McGovern, whose crime-clan surnames were already familiar to our readers. The duo led one of the largest organised shop-lifting gangs in the UK but had never come to public attention. Since exposing the scale and sophistication of their highly organised network, they have rarely been out of the press and their faces have become known to every retail-worker in the land.

Unlike some who fall into the trap of taking sides, I was even-handed in my treatment of the Lyons and the Daniels. In 2008 I unmasked the highly dangerous Daniel mob enforcer Kevin 'Gerbil' Carroll, then aged 27. That first story told how he was suspected of stealing a British army Heckler & Koch sub-machine gun, supplied by rogue soldiers of the Argyll and Sutherland Highlanders. Paul McBride QC later told me he secured Carroll a very favourable plea deal with a Crown prosecutor who mistakenly thought Carroll was merely a 'daft wee boy' despite being branded 'public enemy No. 1' due to his exceptional violence.

That same year came the exposure of Ian Donaldson in a story carefully vetted by lawyers which could not say much beyond that he had once been accused of a gangland kidnapping and was a wannabe racing driver who drove a £150,000 Lamborghini Gallardo against souped-up Fords and Hondas. Years later we could be more expansive after Donaldson – no relation to Frankie 'Donuts' Donaldson – stood trial on major drug-trafficking and money-laundering charges in Spain. A Madrid court heard how this 32-year-old had somehow acquired a £1-million villa in Tenerife and a fleet of luxury cars that included a Ferrari F430 Spider, a Ferrari 599 GTB Fiorano, two Hummers, a Porsche Cayenne Turbo, an Audi Q7, a Mercedes 63 AMG and a couple of BMWs.

Another gangland thug to feel some heat was Craig 'Rob Roy' Gallagher, a one-time crony of Carroll, who I learned had been arrested in connection with his murder. In happier times, the pair were suspected of leading the 'alien abduction gang' who kidnapped and tortured street-dealers in order to extort money and drugs from them. The gang's name came from the traumatised victims being found abandoned half-dressed in the street and claiming not to know what had happened to them. I exposed the gang's terrorising of the criminal underworlds in Glasgow and Edinburgh in 2009.

Perhaps the most bonkers, albeit strangely sinister, crook I dealt with was Giovanni di Stefano, a bogus lawyer who styled himself 'the Devil's Advocate'. With a supposed £450-million fortune, di Stefano claimed to have a bewildering mix of clients including major London organised criminals, serial-killer Dr Harold Shipman, Saddam Hussein and Osama bin Laden. Usefully for him, some of these are not checkable – just like his alleged wealth.

In 1999 he emerged as a 'businessman' poised to come

to the rescue of financially stricken Dundee FC – his interest apparently stemming from his son, who attended Gordonstoun School, the alma mater of Prince Charles. Like Barry Hughes and Paul Ferris, he deployed PR smoke and mirrors but on a global scale, observing Nazi propagandist Joseph Goebbels' maxim that, 'the bigger the lie, the more it will be believed'.

He had first appeared on the public stage in 1992 as part of a bid for Hollywood's MGM Studios which was never taken seriously and resulted in him being forced to leave the US while two associates were jailed. If only we in the Scottish press had seen the comment from studio spokesman Craig Parsons, who told the *Los Angeles Times*: 'We're getting a good chuckle out of all this.' The Dundee bid eventually fell apart in much the same way as his Tinseltown adventure.

Journalist Martin Hannan of *Scotland on Sunday* discovered that di Stefano had been jailed for five years by a court in London in 1986 over a £25-million fraud. The judge said di Stefano was 'one of nature's fraudsters . . . a swindler without scruple or conscience'. Hannan was then subjected to false smears by di Stefano and hollow threats of a €19-million legal action.

The following year I came across two truly startling revelations about di Stefano. The first was an accusation he was bankrolling a savage paramilitary group responsible for 25,000 deaths during the Bosnian war in the 1990s. I unearthed transcripts of evidence from the United Nations war crimes tribunal at The Hague of former Yugoslav president Slobodan Milošević, who died five years into the proceedings, which were never concluded. A protected witness told the court that di Stefano financed his friend Zeljko 'Arkan' Raznatović's Serbian Volunteer Guard, known as the Tigers, which slaughtered

men, women and children. The *Sunday Mail* reported,
'The revelations put di Stefano at the heart of a regime
responsible for some of the worst ethnic cleansing since
the Nazis. He has already spoken out in defence of Adolf
Hitler – last week he said there was "no evidence" to link
him with the Holocaust.'

When I contacted di Stefano, he denied financing the
murderous Tigers but then said he would have done so if
only Arkan had asked him! The following week, I came
across the second revelation – that di Stefano had allegedly attended a high-level summit of the Calabrian Mafia,
known as the 'Ndrangheta, in southern Italy. Magistrates
accused him of being a *'colletto bianco'* or 'white collar'
member at the meeting, which attracted international
Mafioso and two other Mafia groups – Cosa Nostra and
Sacra Corona Unita. Discussions centred around using
terror to seize control of the Italian democratic process.

The highly detailed revelations were made by two
Palermo-based journalists whose book stated, 'This
"colletto bianco" was identified by the magistrates in
Palermo as Giovanni di Stefano, originally from Petrella
Tifernina, Campobasso, who earned the friendship of
ex-Serbian leader Milošević and Željko Raznatović, better
known as Arkan.'

When I contacted di Stefano for the second time, he
was not very pleased to hear from me and blustered that
it was all 'a hundred-per-cent untrue'. A few days later I
received a call from the police in Glasgow. A detective
explained that di Stefano had made a formal complaint
that I had tried to extort money from him. The gist of
di Stefano's nonsensical claim was that I was in cahoots
with some bank with which he had a dispute, and we had
plotted some kind of shakedown. I told the policeman my
revelations about di Stefano, the Serbian murder squads

and an Italian Mafia summit. The bemused officer did not need much persuading that di Stefano's allegation was utter nonsense and did not trouble me again. He should have gone after di Stefano for wasting police time.

Allegations of bankrolling war crimes and terror in Italian politics put di Stefano's fraud conviction into perspective, but these two stories got lost and forgotten as he continued peddling his fiction in newspapers all over the world. But as ancient Chinese general Sun Tzu may have said, 'If you wait by the river long enough, the bodies of your enemies will float by.'

Sure enough, nine years later di Stefano was jailed in London for 14 years for fraud, deception and money-laundering. As he was carted off to his cell, I discovered that he had cooked up a real whopper – that his dad was murdered by British spies – in a desperate bid to cheat justice.

Detective Constable Jerry Walters of City of London Police told me, 'There are no depths he wouldn't have sunk to in order to get off. He said the British security services had murdered his dad with an ice pick because of his own [never proven] involvement with Saddam Hussein. We discovered that his dad did die in Italy, but it was of natural causes. It also emerged that di Stefano only reported the murder allegation in Italy four days before his trial was due to start. So he waited six years after his dad's death, then made a false allegation that he had been murdered to try and get off.'

Exposing gangsters like di Stefano was only a part of what I did as a procession of lawyers, police officers, politicians and businessmen received a short, sharp journalistic shock. If white-collar crooks or rogue cops are not properly dealt with by their chums in authority or benefit from cover-up and collusion, then it falls to journalists

23

SUNRISE

First week in a new job and a £250,000 writ lands on my desk. I suppose that's one way to get noticed. It was a load of cobblers, a vexatious attack from a criminal turned self-styled legal expert called James McDonald – a pound-shop Giovanni di Stefano from Stirling.

Just like di Stefano, this garrulous crook dispenses his own loopy brand of wisdom to a raft of gangster cronies, mostly in connection with Proceeds of Crime cases, and shares the delusion that his ravings are credible. McDonald craves publicity but only on his terms, with a pet reporter recounting respectful tales which airbrush his previous prison sentences dating back to 1965, including a seven-year stretch for handling counterfeit cash.

I had discovered that he was helping paedophile John McCallum, a wealthy member of the traveller community in Edinburgh, to try to overturn a conviction and 10-year jail sentence for abusing two children. My revelations are not the type of publicity that McDonald approves of, so he decided to sue me personally and my new employer, *The Scottish Sun*, for £250,000. A great deal of time and effort were wasted dealing with the matter. My initial memo was almost 700 words long with seven attachments, while the subsequent court defence to McDonald's writ ran to around 1,400 words. He abandoned his claim but we had no hope of recovering costs from a three-time bankrupt. All this for a story with a word count of 187.

I joined *The Scottish Sun* as Investigations Editor in 2014 after taking redundancy from the *Sunday Mail* in order to pay off a personal legal bill that would otherwise have forced me from my home. For all that McDonald's writ was arrant nonsense, its arrival in my first week fed a perception by some that my journalism was risky or cavalier, a magnet for legal problems. Far from it – not a single crook has successfully sued over a single word that I have written. Everything was subjected to suffocating scrutiny. While the US constitution's First Amendment guarantees freedom of speech, in this country the starting point tends to be working out what cannot be reported. Much of my time is spent arguing with media lawyers who are as skittish as thoroughbred racehorses, only more expensive and less predictable.

In my new job I was expected to go after gangsters, politicians, police officers and the inhabitants of Scotland's legal swamp, but the post-Leveson environment has stifled the press and the winners are those with the cash to tie journalism in legal knots. Increasingly, editors are forced to choose the easy path.

My attempt to arrange a straightforward crack cocaine purchase from a Lyons family member became asphyxiated by red tape, forcing its abandonment. Gone were the days when we just went out and did these jobs, such as the heroin buy from the house displaying Coca-Cola festive lights.

There was scope for good old-fashioned gangster unmasking. James 'Jasper' McCann was a nasty piece of work from Glasgow's east end, and I wanted to call him 'Scotland's most dangerous man'. The lawyer allowed 'branded Scotland's most dangerous man'. McCann had walked free from two horrific knife attacks in two years, the justice system having been frustrated when terrified witnesses and victims failed to speak up. I pulled together all the information and approached the victims while a brave photographer secured a pin-sharp picture of McCann's scowling face.

Scottish Labour's murky gangland links remained fruitful. Wide-boy councillor George Redmond bragged in a BBC documentary about his 'big influence' over £1 billion of public spending for the 2014 Commonwealth Games in Glasgow. Others who featured in the show were members of the Faulds family, who have heaped misery on poor residents of Dalmarnock in the city's east end for generations. Brian 'Nightmare' Faulds, murdered prior to broadcast, posthumously showed off bullet and blade scars and bragged about shooting someone. His 'local entrepreneur' brother Darren crowed about getting £65,000 compensation for his three shops being demolished to make way for the Games. Our investigation helpfully pointed out that the billion-pound councillor was related to the Faulds family, this fact having been omitted from the broadcast programme.

Fly-on-the-wall shows about gypsy lifestyles are ubiquitous, but the darker side of the traveller community is out of bounds to TV cameras. I investigated Scotland's largest traveller family, the McPhees, as they waged a cross-border feud with an English group, like *The Dandy* classic comic strip 'The Jocks and the Geordies', although not quite as innocently rib-tickling. The travellers record YouTube videos in which they detail the horrors they intend to inflict on each other. One edgy production, filmed on location in a Lanarkshire scrapyard, sees a crazed McPhee threaten to 'slaughter half of England'. A member of the English

family, wearing a Nazi swastika armband, responds,
'You think Adolf Hitler was a bad man, a really, really
bad man. My word on it – I'm a worser man than Adolf
Hitler.'

I knew I had strayed into serious territory when *The
Digger* news magazine tweeted a warning to me about
criminal travellers being more dangerous than gangsters.
The Digger is a plucky, street-fighting publication despised
by criminals and with a bravely admirable disregard for
those it upsets.

The Daniel versus Lyons drugs war came back on the
agenda with the return of Scotland's unofficial hide-and-
seek champion Billy 'Buff' Paterson after almost five years
on the run in Spain. While Ross Monaghan had been earlier acquitted of the Asda assassination of Kevin 'Gerbil'
Carroll, fugitive Paterson was less fortunate and was jailed
for at least 22 years. I revealed that he only stopped hiding because he had fathered a baby while on the run and
believed he would beat the rap, just like Monaghan. That
both these men and other Lyons mobsters are graduates
of the police-, Labour- and council-backed Chirnsyde
remains a scandal which has never provoked the outrage
or explanation that it merits.

When Carroll was killed in a hail of 13 bullets, the
police and witnesses spoke of there being three men
involved in the murder – two gunmen and a getaway
driver. It occurred to me that no one had ever identified
the driver. I learned that the mystery man was suspected
of being Victor Gallagher, a Lyons relative. Gallagher's
off-radar criminal lifestyle meant that pinning down his
whereabouts was not easy, but I got a break with a possible
address in Cumbernauld, found buried in a court record.
Several tedious days of discretion and patience outside
the property eventually paid off and we surreptitiously

captured the first image of the suspected third member of the Asda hit squad.

As a bonus, I was delighted and surprised when Gallagher received a visitor. It was my first sighting of Steven Lyons since he and Monaghan ran away from me outside the High Court a decade earlier. Lyons had also spent many years in Spain and remains number one target in the Daniels' hit list. He was oblivious to our presence but should have been grateful for being caught in a camera's crosshairs instead of a gunman's.

The legal environment in my new post at *The Scottish Sun* was often stifling. Veteran freelance journalist Eamon O Connor came to me with staggering revelations about the unsolved murder of Glasgow prostitute Emma Caldwell. The police had doggedly pursued a group of Turkish men but they were innocent. Some detectives were more interested in another man. O Connor discovered that my former *Sunday Mail* colleagues were on to the story, which meant that I had less than eight hours to do what should have taken several days, if not weeks. As O Connor drove up from Manchester, I urgently went looking for the other suspect and eventually got him on the phone that Friday afternoon.

I asked if he knew Caldwell and he replied, 'Nope.' I told him that was a lie and that we knew he had used her for sex and had taken police officers to the remote spot where her body was discovered. He said, 'I don't know where you're getting your information from but it's totally wrong. I never was of interest at all. I was told from day one by the police I was never a suspect.'

Our story was written at breakneck speed and put in front of lawyers and various backroom journalists. The lawyers gave us the green light. The story was on the front page, ready to go. But the green light turned amber. Then red. The story was spiked, leaving O Connor and me cursing and deflated. The next day's *Sunday Mail* ran the revelations on page one and another eight inside, which landed them a shiny award, led to a major review of the murder enquiry and triggered a clumsy police attempt to illegally unearth the paper's source.

I suffered similar frustration with a story about bent Edinburgh lawyer Christopher Hales, who had been struck off over 13 dodgy mortgage deals involving an unnamed client, which were worth over £1 million and breached money-laundering regulations. It was written in August 2014 but, despite there being no legal impediment, it was never used. A year later, *The Sunday Times* published the Hales story, with the added ingredient of identifying the mystery client as Michelle Thomson, who had just become an SNP MP. For this, the paper also won a shiny gong.

The failure to publish the Caldwell and Hales stories was hugely frustrating but not unusual – many others I wrote were met with internal resistance, for no apparent good reason.

Another major bugbear I had was the tendency to treat some criminals favourably, or as celebrities, especially those they were on friendly terms with. Paul Ferris received fawning coverage, as did the exiled Loyalist terrorist Johnny 'Mad Dog' Adair, who was portrayed like a reality TV star, not an indiscriminate murderer of people for being Catholic.

Perhaps even worse was the coverage of Barry Hughes, which went against everything I stood for and made me queasy. The first wave of nausea came in June 2014, weeks after I started my new job. A simpering story appeared in which a 'friend' of Hughes told that he had become a dad and revealed the newborn's 'wacky' name. The 'friend' informed concerned readers that 'it's been a tough few months and this is some great news at last' – the 'tough few months' being a sympathetic reference to his convictions for fraud and money-laundering. I muttered about how objectionable it was to treat a criminal like a celebrity, to empathise with the 'tough' ordeal of his chosen path of criminality, but no one was keen to debate my ethical concerns.

A few months later, I ran the story about Hughes and his wife Jackie getting £176,000 of legal aid, then enjoying an opulent Dubai holiday. When bankruptcy quickly followed – with almost £10 million cheated from HMRC – I was surprised to learn that Hughes had been allowed to pick his own trustee.

In February 2015 I produced an investigation into organised crime in Scotland. Run over five days, the subjects included major feuds, the big bosses, the influx of foreign groups and the roles of women. The one dealing with women referred to Hughes and his wife Jackie securing the deal which saw him plead guilty while she walked free, charges dropped. The story explained how the Crown Office was increasingly using this tactic as leverage against men. This was the story that had resulted in the '45 minutes of fury' call from Hughes to my editor, Gordon Smart, and was quickly followed by a lawyer's letter.

The lawyer hired by Hughes was Paul Reid, who also represents Frankie 'Donuts' Donaldson. Reid finds time for his gangland clients between stints sitting on the bench, where he wears a wig and dispenses justice as Sheriff Paul Reid. Reid's letter was not just laughable in its demand for an apology and compensation for Hughes and his wife, but inaccurate. He wrote, 'She [Jackie Hughes] is a lady of impeccable character. She has never come to the attention of the authorities, her reputation in society is considerable. The article is clearly offensive, untrue and defamatory of her substantial reputation.' Never come to the attention of the authorities? In 2010 she appeared in a court dock charged with three counts of fraud and four under the Proceeds of Crime Act. The fraudulent mortgage obtained by her co-accused and husband was taken in her name.

Throughout this period, bankruptcy appeared to have no detrimental impact on Hughes's lavish lifestyle, as evidenced by a drip-feed of stories in *The Scottish Sun*. On one occasion a photographer was told to be in place for Hughes getting into his soft-top black Porsche along with Celtic footballer Anthony Stokes. A photo of the pair of them and the car appeared with the headline 'ANT'S A TOP CAR BARRY' but no mention of bankruptcy.

The next story about Hughes saw him on a Barbados beach, wide toothy grin and hands in pockets, chatting to Manchester United and England star Wayne Rooney. Under the headline 'HUGHES LOOKIN' AT ROO', it told how the pair 'happily nattered as their kids played together in the sea'. Any casual reader would assume Hughes was an urbane, successful businessman – not a two-bob bankrupt thug with gangland connections. The story read like a 'Wish you were here?' postcard to the folks back home until the final line, which made a fleeting reference to Hughes being fined for mortgage fraud, although, yet again, the piece failed to mention the active bankruptcy.

Even the most simple, slavish, naive or incompetent journalist should have raised the blindingly obvious question: how is it possible that a bankrupt owing £10 million to the tax man, whose every penny is supposedly under the control of a court-appointed trustee, is able to swan around on a luxury Caribbean holiday? I was sickened.

Hughes was a major figure of interest due to his criminality and associates. He had attacked me and the newspaper through legal channels. Yet he was still able to click his fingers and demand soft-soap treatment.

If no one else was bothered about it, I was. Days after the Rooney story, I emailed his trustee to say, 'You may also be aware that Mr Hughes' lifestyle does not appear to have been impeded by his sequestration, as he continues to be seen in expensive vehicles and exotic locations. If your investigation in this case results in the need for the sequestration being extended, I would be grateful if you could let me know.'

There was no reply, and my workplace protestations about this perverse PR fell on deaf ears. Weeks after the Barbados photo, *The Scottish Sun* carried a story about one of Hughes's daughters raising money for charity with her 'glitzy birthday party'. It reported: 'She was joined by celebrity guests including Towie star Lauren Pope, 33, as well as Celtic striker Anthony Stokes and Rangers ace Nicky Law, both 27. Following the event at the city's trendy St Jude's bar, her dad Barry, 36, said: "It's a great gesture for a really good cause and we're extremely proud of her."' How generous! Staging a grandstanding charity birthday bash while owing the tax man £10 million. It was taking the public, including our readers, for mugs. Of course, this puff piece contained no mention of criminality or bankruptcy but did include the name of his daughter's private school, the fees for which Hughes was somehow able to pay. I did not see the story at the time – which is just as well. Had I done so, my reaction might not have been conducive to office harmony or career progression.

24

DEFIANCE AND BETRAYAL

After a helter-skelter of doctors, Christmas, aching eyes, burning skin, Hogmanay, hobbling, racing thoughts, restless nights, tears and a mobile phone seemingly possessed came a conversation that stopped me in my tracks. It was 16 days since the acid attack when I called my boss Gordon Smart to tell him that Frankie 'Donuts' Donaldson was due in court.

Still reeling from the discovery that Donaldson wrongly believed me to be in a relationship with his ex-partner Jane Clarke, I realised that, rather than back down, the only option was to stand firm. Smart agreed with my suggestion of press solidarity and alerting all newspapers to Donaldson's spurious £1-million claim against Jane, which was nothing but an extension of his campaign of domestic terror and control.

He then brought up the phone call of 10 months prior, the obstreperous whining from Barry Hughes about my 'GIRL POWER' investigation detailing the roles of women in organised crime. Smart told me what I already knew – that Hughes had been angry because we dared publish details about him and his wife and their criminal saga, even thought every word was accurate.

What Smart said next caused me to freeze, incredulous. According to Smart, Hughes hadn't just vented – he had also revealed knowledge about my car, home address and other personal information and that harm would be done to me. I was so taken aback that I did not ask why on earth this had been withheld from me until now. Even before Smart dropped this bombshell, I had deemed the Hughes call concerning enough to include in my letter, posted the day before, to Greater Glasgow CID boss Detective Superintendent Stevie Grant. I was reeling. Why had Smart not told me at the time? I am certain there was no malice on his part. The only conclusion that made any sense was that he had not viewed the Hughes call as a serious threat. Perhaps the newspaper's favourable relationship with Hughes was also a factor in not mentioning it at the time. But why tell me now? Had Smart simply forgotten that he had withheld it? It seemed to be the only logical explanation. I wanted to know exactly what Hughes had said. More pressingly, I hoped that Smart would provide Detective Sergeant Craig Warren with every single detail.

I immediately sent Smart a text, ostensibly confirming the plan to alert other editors to the Donaldson case, but adding, 'In my letter to cops I mentioned the BH [Barry Hughes] call to you last March [actually February] but I wasn't aware that he knew my address, car & reg, ex-wife info etc. or that he was making actual threats. Given what's happened I think it would be worthwhile telling cops everything about that call.'

I called DS Warren to pass on the new details about the Hughes call, then emailed the Solicitor General, Lesley Thomson, who had taken a personal interest in my well-being. I told her, 'Mr Smart today informed me that during that call, Mr Hughes made a clear threat to harm me and told him my home address, car make and registration and other personal details. I have suggested to Mr Smart that Police Scotland ought to be given a full statement about what was said by Mr Hughes.'

It was 27 days and 17 medical appointments after the attack when I returned to work, determined and defiant. It is not in my nature to hide away with the curtains closed. It was business as usual. I also had matters to address with my editor, the police, the judiciary and the Crown.

When I arrived in the office, trainers cushioning my aching feet, I passed the desk of a senior executive who beamed: 'It's not the first time some bloke has splashed liquid on your face.' Beside him, Smart chimed: 'I hope you've got plenty of stories.' I did not expect a brass band and ticker tape, nor am I a weeping wallflower, but the tone felt slightly unnecessary.

Smart did not come near me for the rest of the day so, the following day, I sent him an email to try and get some answers. I wrote, 'One aspect of it [the Barry Hughes call] I didn't fully take on board was his reference to my ex-wife/divorce. It surprises and troubles me that he had that info and I would like to find out who told him. I'd be really grateful if you could recall what he said as that will enable me to ask questions of various people who had knowledge of my divorce.' Just like my text message, no reply was forthcoming. It seemed the editor had decided it would be smart to clam up.

That same day, I sent a letter to Scotland's most senior judge, Lord Carloway, a lawyer called Colin Sutherland, whose full title is Lord President of the Court of Session and Lord Justice General of the High Court of Justiciary. I wanted to prevent any chance of my attacker William 'Basil' Burns coming in front of Sheriff Paul Reid, who as a lawyer had also represented Donaldson, Hughes and other criminals I had dealt with. I believed that Carloway should know that Reid was acting for Donaldson in the £1-million civil case against Jane, and that the domestic violence case was contaminated with threats towards witnesses. I explained about Reid's letter of complaint to my newspaper on behalf of Hughes and his wife, and the sheriff's inaccurate claim that she 'has never come to the attention of the authorities'. The letter concluded, 'Given the claims made by Mr Reid on behalf of clients such as these, I have concerns about his suitability as a judicial office holder but appreciate that is a matter for yourself and the Judicial Appointments Board for Scotland. However, given the above, I would greatly appreciate it if you could ensure that Mr Reid has no involvement in the proceedings involving my assailant Mr Burns.'

Being aware of the judiciary's hostility to any perceived criticism from outsiders, coupled with their entrenched culture of secrecy, I did not expect much back. I was not disappointed. Carloway's legal secretary, Roddy Flinn, told me that Reid is 'entitled to represent his client's version of events', adding, 'There is no suggestion in your letter that Mr Reid acted irresponsibly in so writing.'

Wrong. This prompted me to respond with another letter, more forthright in tone. I wrote:

> I respectfully disagree with Mr Flinn's interpretation of my letter of January 20. It is obviously proper for a solicitor to faithfully represent a client's version of events where instructions are honest and reasonable. However, Mr Reid's decision to knowingly make a false statement on behalf of this client (Mrs Jackie Hughes) is irresponsible, dishonest, unprofessional and improper. I believe that such conduct is incompatible with the high standards apparently

expected of judicial office in Scotland. I find it concerning that a part-time sheriff, while being well remunerated through public funds, is free to simultaneously act in an aggressive and/or dishonest manner on behalf of major organised criminals.

Back came another reply from Flinn, proposing that I could raise my concerns about Reid's lawyerly conduct with his professional body, the Law Society of Scotland. This would be futile, of course, knowing as I did the Law Society to be a trade body and aggressive lobbyist for its members, not a fair and independent arbiter for the public.

In response to Flinn's question of whether I was complaining about Reid's conduct as a judge, I replied:

My knowledge of the judicial complaint process causes me to believe that making a complaint may be ineffective due to a lack of fairness and transparency. Given the detailed concerns that I have raised about Mr Reid's dishonest conduct in his dual and conflicting roles, I would respectfully suggest that what happens next is your decision to make.

I would be grateful if you could inform me of your decision. As previously stated, I would gladly provide any information that may be required.

And that marked the end of my correspondence with the judiciary.

Back at work, I tried to get on with my job, but the niggle about Smart was ever present. I confided in a colleague who was aghast and urged me to raise the matter officially, but instigating an internal grievance process was the last thing I needed.

Two CID officers came to the office for a statement from Smart, with a company lawyer at his side. This took two visits as they ran out of time – hardly instilling confidence in me that they were doing anything other than going through the motions about who was behind the attack.

On the same day as the CID's first visit to Smart, there was a breakthrough in the acid attack investigation. Alex Porter, the getaway driver who had roared away without his hitman passenger, was detained. I did not know Porter's name, let alone anything about him, which indicated his lowly position in gangland's pecking order. The day after Porter's detention, I was surprised when a member of the company's HR department asked me to provide them with information about Smart's undisclosed Hughes phone call, having apparently learned of it from the colleague whose confidence I sought.

Later that same day I got a call from DS Warren. He said he wanted to see me but would only tell me what it was about in person. He came to the office and warned me there was intelligence suggesting that my safety could be at risk. Such a warning is known as a 'threat to life' or an 'Osman' after the London businessman Ali Osman, who was murdered in 1988 when the police had failed to disclose a threat from his killer.

The police required me to sign a document acknowledging receipt of the warning. It felt like a legal hand-washing exercise should I end up injured or dead. A jarring section of the template document says the warning 'does not justify you committing any criminal acts'. Gangsters involved in feuds frequently receive Osmans, hence the warning not to retaliate, but the only retaliation I planned involved the legal use of written words, not guns and knives. When I told the company about the Osman, they went into a minor meltdown. The acid attack had shaken senior management in London and Glasgow, and there was a reassuring willingness to do whatever was needed to ensure my safety. They suggested numerous times that I could temporarily leave the country or even ensconce myself in some kind of safe house. Would I at least consider personal security guards to accompany me and be discreetly placed outside my home? Er, no thanks – I'm a journalist not the President of the United States.

I politely declined these extreme offers but did agree to the use of a hire car as I was conscious that my own vehicle was known, and that I was at my most vulnerable while travelling between work and home. This went on for weeks but the novelty of being on first-name terms with Hertz staff quickly wore off and the final hire vehicle was returned.

Keen to assess the significance of the Osman, I contacted Labour MSP and former police chief Graeme Pearson, who counselled that the police would be 'hyper-sensitive' about my wellbeing because of my job, joking that journalists were a 'fairly precious commodity', several levels above MSPs.

A James Bond-style gadget arrived on my desk. It looked like a chunky black car-key fob but was in fact a panic button. When pressed, it would transmit an audio of what was happening in the immediate vicinity to an operator who could call 999, directing the police through the device's GPS. The gizmo needed to be charged daily and soon ended up in the back of the kitchen junk drawer. 007 never had such problems.

I was at work on Saturday, 6 February 2016, when I picked up a police press release about the arrest of a man for the non-fatal shooting of the Daniel family associate Ross Sherlock, who was targeted outside a primary school in suburban Bishopbriggs. The police do not name arrested people – they only provide their age. But I was immediately curious as the alleged school shooter was 58 – the same age as acid-attacker Burns. My curiosity was heightened because of Burns's links to the Lyons mob through his Paisley associate Robert 'Piggy' Pickett – ergo an enemy of Daniel associates such as Sherlock.

I simultaneously contacted the CID office dealing with my attack and the press officer who issued the release, asking them both the same question. A coy CID officer came back quickest, confirming that, yes, it was Burns who had been charged with the shooting. I was annoyed with the police for failing to inform me of this massive development and equally peeved when my by-line was removed from the story, which felt like an act of cowardice. In an emailed request to the duty editor, which was rebuffed, I said, 'To run scared and change how I do things is exactly what these people want. I would like respectfully to ask that my name be put back on the story. This is not to make any big point but to show these people that it is business as usual. I wrote this story prior to establishing Burns's identity.'

Smart was rarely seen in the office, and I had pretty much lost hope of him providing me with my request for details of the Hughes call. HR boss Emily Bayne called me in for a chat. I expressed sincere gratitude to her and senior management for their support but disappointment that Smart had not even replied to the email I had sent him three weeks earlier. She said she would tell him to do so.

That day at work was full tilt. A bloodbath gun attack had taken place at a Dublin boxing weigh-in between two rival drug gangs and I established a Scottish link. Glasgow lawyer Sam Kynoch was the boss of MGM Scotland, a gym and promotions company that was the 'sister business' of a Marbella gym run by the Kinahan mob, one of the factions in the Irish gang war.

As I was up to my neck in phone calls about the lawyer and the Dublin drug war, Smart came over and invited me into his private office. The tone was courteous and civil – I sought answers, not an argument. I asked him for every detail of what Hughes had said to him as it might have had some bearing on the acid attack. It might also have helped work out how such sensitive personal information had reached Hughes.

Smart told me that Hughes was 'quite specific' about getting me 'done in' and 'reeled off a list of things' about me. According to Smart, Hughes had 'done research' on me and had 'taken an interest in a lot of the detail about' me. Disappointingly, Smart struggled to recall the specifics – which would have been fresher had he told me at the time. Furthermore, Hughes allegedly said he could not 'lay a finger' on Smart, as he was the editor, but did say, 'I'm going to hurt your friends.'

Smart revealed that he personally brokered the Hughes story about the Barbados beach and Wayne Rooney – which made no mention of Hughes being a £9.6 million bankrupt.

As I listened silently agog, Smart also revealed that he made the Hughes call 'go away' with the following suggestion: 'Why don't you send a legal letter and Russell will be disciplined?' So the time-consuming complaint from Sheriff Paul Reid, with its falsehoods about Jackie Hughes, seems to have been instigated by my own editor to make a criminal think it would land me in trouble!

Smart explained his connection with Hughes by saying it was inherited from his predecessor David Dinsmore, who had just been promoted to the post of Chief Operating Officer of News UK. I first met Dinsmore as a schoolboy doing work experience at the local paper where he was a young reporter. Upon becoming editor, Smart claimed to have phoned Dinsmore to say, 'Barry's telling me you're his best friend,' and that Hughes had been a good source of stories for him. The dynamic of the Dinsmore–Hughes relationship was described by Smart as 'Michelle Mone 2' – a reference to lingerie tycoon and Tory peer Michelle Mone and her hunger for self-publicity.

I left Smart's office with an explanation but no apology. As I numbly returned to my desk, I felt betrayed and conflicted. Should I make a fuss or keep my mouth shut? A cool head was required. The situation was unlike anything I had experienced. Life was still consumed by the attack and its aftermath and I was acutely conscious that doing nothing was better than doing the wrong thing. Little did I know, it would ultimately lead to my departure from my job.

That Sunday's paper carried my investigation revealing the Kinahan gang's foothold in Scotland under the front-page headline 'COPS PROBE "IRISH MAFIA" FIGHT NIGHTS'. I was happy to provide a smaller story with background information about the sport's deep links to criminality, which I saw as an opportunity to reset *The Scottish Sun*'s troubling relationship with Hughes, by hopefully extinguishing his orchestrated and perverse portrayal as a figure of success, celebrity and legitimacy. The story began:

> Scotland's fight game has long been tainted by hoods and heavies. Thug promoter Barry Hughes, 37, is a crony of feared gangland boss Jamie 'Iceman' Stevenson, 50. Hughes, of Kilmacolm,

Renfrewshire, courts publicity as a self-styled business tycoon.

But he has a string of convictions for violence, fraud, money laundering and carrying a knife.

Two years ago he enjoyed a £50,000 Dubai holiday weeks before he went bust owing the tax man £9.8million.

When another groundless letter from Sheriff Paul Reid arrived on my desk, I burst out laughing.

25

SUNSET

Slinking out of *The Scottish Sun* office for an appointment with my GP one regular Wednesday morning, I had no idea that I would not return. Not that day, not ever. It's not that I was at breaking point. I had already broken – it just took me a while to realise.

Prior to the acid attack, I was dealing with an array of emotional personal issues. When William 'Basil' Burns came to my door, as strange as it may sound, the frenetic aftermath felt like a welcome distraction from those pains. Of course, this was illusory as the attack only added to the pressure on me.

The immediate and intense consequences of a knife-wielding, fake postman splashing sulphuric acid in my face became all-consuming. My mind was alive and fizzing with anxious thoughts, regrets and unanswerable questions. What if my daughter had answered the door to Burns? What if his knife had found my guts? Should I have inflicted real damage on Burns? What was to be done about those who sent him? Why were the police sitting on their hands?

Dark winter nights and mornings put me in a state of high alert while coming and going from my home. Strange cars and unknown faces were clocked, registration numbers scrawled down. Every approaching person in the street was instantly assessed, my fists clenched as I asked: were their hands in or out of pockets?, faces covered or visible?, benign or malign?, fight or flee?

Friends and family rallied round. I smiled and nodded, got back to work. Good old-fashioned defiance and stoicism. Everything is fine, I insisted. I wasn't lying – just kidding myself and them. When I then discovered that Gordon Smart had withheld the alleged Barry Hughes threat, yet another front opened in my already too busy, crazily cluttered mind. Initially dumbstruck, I then demanded answers. When I sat in Smart's office and finally elicited the full technicolour details, I could only hope he would be as candid with the CID.

Over the following days and weeks, I caught occasional glimpses of Smart, but we had no reason to communicate and he seemed to keep a wary distance.

My initial feelings of shock, hurt and betrayal mutated and hardened into bitterness, mistrust and anger. What might I say or do if I came face-to-face with Smart in a corridor or lift? As it turned out, we would never speak again. He vanished from the Glasgow office. Promoted to the post of deputy editor in London, he unexpectedly left the company eight months later.

I confided in two colleagues whose judgements I value. One arched his eyebrows and murmured, 'You have got to be fucking kidding!' while the other, eyes darting round the newsroom, rhetorically asked, 'How can you possibly trust them again?'

I kept getting drawn back to the collection of obsequious, pro-Hughes stories which served to fuel my anger and growing conviction that my uncompromising style of journalism was incompatible with the newspaper I worked for. Other friends and fellow journalists, measured and sensible people, were even more scathing. Their disgust helped reassure me that my feelings were entirely appropriate. The following words from *Shōgun*, James Clavell's classic novel about 16th-century feudal Japan, describe my situation: 'A man has a false heart in his mouth for all the world to see, another in his breast to show his very special friends and his family, and the real one, the true one, the secret one, which is never known to anyone except himself alone.' The world saw the façade of a bold and defiant journalist, my friends and family were privy to the emotions beneath the surface, but only I knew that neither of these were anything like the full truth. Following Smart's revelation, I managed to hold it together for just over five weeks. I finally admitted that I was unwell and in need of help. When I sat in front of my GP, feeling strangely guilty for slipping away from my desk, a jumble of words came tumbling from my mouth and a garden sprinkler appeared behind my eyes. So that's why doctors have a box of tissues to hand.

While some men are reluctant to seek such help due to misplaced machismo, the stigma of perceived weakness, it was the only sensible option, if not for my mental and physical welfare then for my incredible, inspirational, loving daughter who deserved her real dad back. To my surprise, the GP decreed that I was not fit for work for a period of six weeks minimum. Deep down, I knew she was right, but the prognosis sat uneasily with me. Six weeks sounded like forever. Was it not slightly over the top – a bit of an unnecessary fuss? It's not that I was 'ill' – not really.

Lunchtime was spent enjoyably alone in a café, giving me time to pause for reflection, allowing the new reality to sink in. My GP had prescribed peace, space and time for recovery, to repair and stabilise my erratic emotions. I embraced the opportunity. Knowing that keeping physically and mentally active was vital, I completed a ridiculously lengthy to-do list of DIY tasks, exercised, saw friends and went on excursions.

As I sipped coffee, I had no idea that there would be no return to *The Scottish Sun* or that the novelty and necessity of six weeks of breathing space would evolve into a suffocating state of limbo. Sick leave evolved into garden leave, then a protracted discussion about the terms of my departure.

For 23 years solid I had been a newspaper journalist. It defined me. Week after week, as instructed by my old managing editor, Malcolm Speed, I hunted down stories while others chose the gentler path of tinkering with other people's words, opining or drawing boxes on computer screens. For almost a quarter of a century, life was a machine-gun rat-tat-tat of punchy investigations and exciting exclusives, of unmasking the dangerous, exposing the hypocrites and standing up to the powerful – not to mention miles upon miles of flimflam and filler. Now, at the behest of my GP, it all stopped.

Little did I also know how extraordinary 2016 would become, as I rose like a phoenix from the ashes of a tawdry doorstep acid attack. I met the woman with whom I will spend the rest of my life. I exercised more, I drank less alcohol. I learned to be more appreciative of simple pleasures. I strove to be a better person – more patient and tolerant. I was free to holiday wherever and whenever fancy took me – budget dependent, of course. OK, none of these consequences had been the intention of Burns or his paymaster, but it would be churlish of me not to express my gratitude, even though I did chuckle upon hearing that Burns was continually being shunted around prisons because there was a price on his head.

The gnawing uncertainty of my professional future

meant that being off work was not all a holiday camp and the kitchen calendar continued to be marked with medical appointments, although they gradually petered out. My recovery was vital, as I needed to be fit and alert to deal with the ever-present spectre of the criminal investigation and prosecution of Burns and his getaway driver, Alex Porter.

Burns called on his favourite solicitor. A Crown official informed me that this brief wanted access to my house for the supposed purpose of preparing his client's defence. The thought of him poking around my home made my blood boil. The Crown employee said he was 'flabbergasted' at the lawyer's request and he was duly ordered to stay away.

My only recourse was to raise the matter with the Scottish Legal Complaints Commission, the 'independent' gateway body for complaints about lawyers. Believing it to be pointless, other than for the purpose of creating an official record, I told them, 'I would like the SLCC to ascertain whether ————'s request was, as I suspect, ordered by Mr Burns (or his associates) in an attempt to intimidate me.' The response from the SLCC was asinine. I had been explicit. I wanted them to investigate *why* the lawyer had sought access to my home but they somehow interpreted this as a request to find out *how* he had got my address. Obviously, he would have had the address all along.

I replied:

> The SLCC is viewed as lacking independence from solicitors and their trade body the Law Society of Scotland. The SLCC's track record suggests it does not have the power or desire to act in the best interests of the public. Your failure to understand a simple letter confirms my beliefs.

> Your letter also makes it clear that the SLCC has
> no interest in considering serious concerns about
> the welfare of me and my family. Therefore, fur-
> ther involvement with the SLCC in relation to this
> matter would be time-consuming and pointless.

When Burns and Porter were also charged with the shooting of the Daniel mob associate Ross Sherlock outside a primary school, it was a complication I could have done without.

Chronic delays and ineptitude are the norm in Scotland's outdated and self-serving prosecution and court system, so I was hardly surprised when the trial was set for 4 January 2017 – more than a year after the event. What really stuck in my craw was that the Crown Office was cynically using my open-and-shut case to support their shaky prosecution of the school shooting and their obvious lack of interest in going after those who ordered the acid attack. Whatever evidence they had against Burns and Porter for the shooting, it would be nowhere near as compelling as that for my attack and probably not enough to prosecute in isolation. If Burns had faced only my charge, the sensible option would be a guilty plea, not least to spare him the embarrassing ordeal of everyone hearing how Scotland's worst hitman was battered then rescued by the police.

I met with two Crown Office people to go through my evidence. They asked about the knife. Again, I answered truthfully that I had not seen it in my attacker's hands. They gave me an undertaking that they would not call my daughter as a witness but asked for her to provide a taped interview to the police. This was agreed to. The meeting ended with a cheery request not to get murdered before the trial as this might make the case trickier to prosecute.

On the day my daughter and I came back from our summer holiday, a clinical psychologist from the State Hospital at Carstairs phoned me on the instruction of the Crown. He asked when it would be possible to speak with my daughter, in order in assess how best she could give her evidence. No, I explained, that was incorrect – the Crown had pledged not to call her. Angered by the failure to even inform me of their changed plan, I emailed them. Back came the reply that there had 'been a misunderstanding' and that 'no undertaking was given by them that [my] daughter would not be called as witness'.

I was no innocent, knowing more than most about the Crown's capacity for flannel, but this falsehood was so unnecessary and served only to destroy any residual trust I had in them. What had actually happened was that the original undertaking had been made without the knowledge or consent of Richard Goddard, the advocate prosecuting the case, and that he, understandably, wanted to keep all options open. If only they had just admitted that, perhaps some goodwill could have been recovered.

The situation deteriorated further. My priority was always to minimise my daughter's exposure to the whole sordid business, while being willing to do whatever was reasonably required to assist the prosecution. The psychologist, having met my daughter, recommended that she should give her evidence 'on commission'. This would mean the she would be filmed, under oath, but prior to the main trial, with a judge, prosecutors and defence lawyers. Burns and Porter would watch on a video link, although the Crown initially failed to disclose this significant fact.

I was not pleased but, for the sake of justice, consented. The Crown proposed this session should take place in Edinburgh, on a school day in November. Why not Glasgow, I asked? Surely they should aim to minimise the impact on a child witness? Was it because an Edinburgh judge might not be agreeable to a trip to Glasgow, even by chauffeur-driven judicial car?

My daughter was not going to miss a day's education and traipse to Edinburgh in order to undergo a challenging and unpleasant ordeal which could just as easily be held close to home. As it happened, the November date was scrapped when one of the defence lawyers claimed they could not make it, so the Crown came up with a new one – 20 December. The timing could not have been worse. My daughter's previous Christmas had been defined by the horror of seeing me attacked. Now the Crown thought it was acceptable to stir up those memories by subjecting her to questioning and cross-examination about the attack, just days from the first anniversary. She deserved a normal Christmas, not a painful re-run of the previous one. Anyway, I wondered, why had they not sorted this out sooner, given they'd had a year to do so.

Through gritted teeth, I reluctantly agreed to the new date because I feared that rejecting it could risk the trial being delayed, but I refused to go to Edinburgh as I knew commission sessions took place in Glasgow.

The Crown compromise was for my daughter to give evidence by a video link from Glasgow while the judge and the rest of them sat in Edinburgh. I agreed but noted bitterly in an email: 'I am disappointed that my daughter's interests appear to be secondary to the convenience of staff and/or the judge involved in this process.'

All we could do now was wait for our days in court.

26

PANTO SEASON

Attending a festive pantomime was the perfect preparation for my long-awaited big date at the High Court in Glasgow. It was the dark days of early January 2017 when, in a brightly lit room, I was reunited with William 'Basil' Burns, who sat in the dock with his sidekick Alex Porter, who I did not recognise.

I spent the morning of 4 January, my birthday, listening to a ticking clock in a windowless beige witness room having already waited more than a year for the show to begin. By lunchtime, someone decided that all the witnesses could go home with an instruction to return the following morning.

That night, two police officers came to my door with a message from the Crown telling me not to attend the next day but could not say why. This turned out to be not the case but no explanation was ever given.

As I went about my business the next morning, a panicked call came from the Crown asking where I was because the curtain was about to go up and I had top billing as witness number one. I explained about the police visit and that I was half an hour away and scruffily dressed, which was met with palpable terror, only allayed by my offer to get there as soon as possible after a quick change of clothes.

Led into court by a costume-clad macer, I stepped into the witness stand.

Burns, hardly bursting with vitality last time we met, had selected a grey suit to match the waxy pallor of his prison tan. He and Porter, who was on bail, sat side by side and appeared less threatening than a pair of pantomime ugly sisters. I met Burns's neutral gaze but did not glower too hard or too long, lest the 15 jurors mistakenly thought I was the villain.

Judge Sean Murphy QC played it straight while the cast of legal-aid-funded lawyers provided humour with their one-liners and overacting. Burns's advocate, Thomas Ross, was naturally but unintentionally comedic, lifting his horse-hair wig as frequently as Laurel and Hardy do their bowler hats.

Having taken the oath, I was walked through the morning of the acid attack in baby steps, prosecutor Richard Goddard's gentle questions yielding a detailed chronology of events. The macer passed me bagged items of evidence including the Royal Mail jacket and the serrated steak knife, enclosed in a plastic tube. Large TV screens flashed up photos of my street and home, my acid-splattered face and hallway and a close-up of the postman's snapped dentures in a pool of dark blood.

Could I see my attacker in court? Like in the movies, a 'follow that car' moment, I slowly pointed my finger at Burns, who gazed back emotionless.

Serious stuff over, it was the turn of Ross. In the immediate days after the attack, I had heard Burns was trying to save face about his sore face by regaling prison pals with the fantastical tale that I had blackmailed him, invited him to my house and then attacked him. I genuinely believed that his fairytale would stay behind bars but, to my astonishment, it formed the basis of his defence.

Ross asked what I would say to the suggestion that I had a photo of Burns in a clinch with a woman who was not his partner and that I was using it to get information from him. What would I say – Are you out of your mind?

I suddenly became conscious of the jurors gazing right at me. My God, they might actually swallow this stuff. I denied it as naturally and calmly as possible, trying not to splutter, bluster or guffaw in case it was perceived as protesting too much.

During his 12 months in prison, Burns had cooked up another layer of lies on top of this nonsense. What, I was asked, if the jury was to hear from another witness called Sean Alexander who could say that I had demanded he give me a phone number for Burns? Apparently, this would be because I was seeking information about a particular murder (a murder I had never even heard of). I flatly replied that it was completely untrue, later wishing I'd added that if Alexander planned to say this under oath, he would be committing perjury.

The defence case unfolded further. As Burns was underneath me and surrounded by witnesses when the police arrived, it would have been impossible to argue that he had not been there. With a flourish, Ross put it to me: 'Mr Burns does not dispute he was the person at your door, but he will tell the jury there was no liquid, no delivery card, no knife.'

Again stifling the instinct to snigger or react with a volley of incredulous expletives, I replied, 'He was wearing a Royal Mail uniform, had a delivery card and threw acid – if that's the best you can come up with, then good luck with that.' My impudence earned a ticking off from Ross, who sniffed that it was the prosecutor's job to question his defence and address the jury, not mine. That was me told.

The lawyer also reeled off each of the injuries suffered by Burns, which caused me to brighten when I learned that he needed some stitches on his chin from my citizen's arrest. If this was to hint I had been too rough towards his client, I suppressed the urge to express regret at not doing any real and permanent damage.

During two hours of questioning and cross-examination, I recalled my humiliating question, 'Why did they send a fat clown like you as a hitman. Is this all I'm worth?' – a soundbite which gave a nice line for stalwart reporter Wilma Riley of the court press agency – but I forgot other snippets which seemed important at the time yet would surely have made no difference given how desperate the defence was. I was free to go.

The next witness was my daughter. After months of being misled and messed around by the Crown, she had been due to give her evidence 'on commission' but, at the 11th hour, the defence conceded it was not necessary and that her police interview would suffice. This was not due to any outbreak of decency but pure pragmatism. While her taped police interview was damaging to the defence, there was a risk that formal testimony could backfire by being even worse. It was a case of the defence deciding to stick or twist, and they stuck.

I went straight from the stand to the public seats to watch the video of my daughter's police interview. Her articulate account elicited a mix of heart-bursting pride and dark anger towards Burns and Porter. She said, 'It caused the biggest fright of my life. All I could think about was my dad. I was crying and I couldn't stop.'

There was a flash of humour when the hushed court heard about her seeing 'this thing' on top of her dad. The 'thing' sat blinking in the dock. One damning recollection was her hearing Burns ask me to sign the Royal Mail delivery card, punching a hole in the defence position that he had turned up without it, the bottle of acid or the knife.

That night there was another episode of inexplicable Crown behaviour. They sent two more police officers with the message that my daughter was required to attend court to give evidence after all. It actually crossed my mind that these might have been fake cops from some kind of hidden camera TV show. It was about the only credible explanation for such crass misinformation one night after a similar experience. On both occasions, the police were blameless – just following Crown orders. I emailed the Crown to say, 'I do not know whether these two episodes of misinformation are due to incompetence or something more serious.' But they did not provide any explanation.

A major problem for the defence was the 'Wee Jamie sends his regards' comment. This had to be denied by Burns in order to maintain the big lie that he had been invited to my home. Ross had already pushed me on this to no avail and suffered another blow when two of my neighbours both recalled Burns saying it.

Over the following two weeks, the jurors heard from more than a dozen other witnesses. A police officer who dragged Burns away from me told how he was wearing surgical gloves underneath a black pair and had just £3.05 cash and no keys or public transport tickets on him. An eye doctor said I could have lost my sight if it had not been for neighbours quickly fetching a basin of water to rinse away the acid. A chemist confirmed sulphuric acid was the substance used, while a forensic expert said the DNA of Burns was on the Royal Mail jacket and that a pair of glasses inside the mail bag had his and Porter's DNA on them. Damningly, Porter's DNA was also found on the handle of the knife. Had it not been, the defence might well have suggested I was wielding it when I answered the door in my pyjama bottoms.

The trial took a dramatic turn with a jaw-dropping revelation. Burns and Porter had been under surveillance by an elite police unit at the time of the acid attack. At any one time between 29 October 2015 and 25 January 2016, up to seven organised crime and counter terrorism officers were tracking the pair's movements. The day before the acid attack, CCTV footage showed what appeared to be Porter's gold Volvo driving near my home at 8.30 a.m. on an apparent reconnaissance run. It was 10 minutes later that the surveillance team got into place around the Paisley addresses of Burns and Porter. At 9.28 a.m. they watched Porter driving the Volvo along Paisley's Greenhill Road. Moments after that, Burns got out of the car and went into a shop before walking towards the street where he lived. The next day, the surveillance officers began their operation at 9 a.m. Too late. Burns and Porter had already left for the day for the same destination as before. Half an hour before the surveillance team began its shift, Burns had thrown acid in my face.

I was not surprised that Burns and Porter were meriting expensive and intensive surveillance, but my head was spinning with 'what ifs'. What if the surveillance officers had been in place earlier? What if they had followed Burns and Porter to my home the day before the attack? Would they have realised what was being planned? Could it have been averted? What if the police team had tracked them on the day of the hit? Would they have foiled Burns before he even reached my door?

When the prosecution of the acid attack ended, it was a Friday and time to hear evidence of the primary school shooting of the Daniel mob associate Ross Sherlock. After the macer's call for Sherlock went unanswered, the judge sent everyone home for the weekend.

That same day, a strange figure was seen loitering outside a primary school in Penilee, Glasgow. A concerned parent filmed the man, who was pushing a buggy but drawing suspicion by his furtive behaviour and the fact that his face was completely hidden by a scarf.

On Monday the macer again called for Sherlock, but he was nowhere to be seen. Another Crown witness was also missing. Later that day, the masked buggy-pushing man was back outside the school. Mirroring the attack on Sherlock, he pulled out a gun and shot a parent collecting his child. The victim was Lyons gang member Ross Monaghan – cleared of the Asda assassination of Kevin 'Gerbil' Carroll, the Daniel henchman and a close friend of Sherlock.

Back in court, the judge was left with no option but to abandon the trial. The past two weeks of evidence had counted for nothing. The time of 15 jurors; the cost to taxpayers of four defence lawyers, a prosecutor, court staff and a judge; the time, inconvenience and stress endured by around 15 witnesses – all a complete waste of time and money.

I learned of the unfolding debacle from a court contact. There then followed a sheepish phone call from the Crown. I hung up in contempt when they refused to identify the AWOL witnesses, who I knew to be Sherlock and another man.

The next day, in desperation and disgust, I wrote to Lord Advocate James Wolffe QC, the head of the Crown Office, to complain that the simple prosecution of Burns for the acid attack had been complicated by the decision to pair it with the school shooting of Ross Sherlock. Given Sherlock's blatant disregard for conventional justice, I urged Wolffe to consider separating the two cases. I wrote, 'Had Mr Burns been prosecuted for my crime alone, he would have almost certainly been convicted, perhaps even without the need for a trial. Myself – and other witnesses – were cynically used by the Crown in order to prop up a shooting case which cannot be prosecuted in isolation due to sparsity of evidence.' It took over two months to receive a reply on behalf of Wolffe. In the meantime, Sherlock had been tracked down and remanded in prison. In mealy-mouthed language, the Crown said the trial debacle was merely 'regrettable' and rejected my request to prosecute the crimes separately.

The festive panto had been a costly dress rehearsal – just another episode of high farce in Scotland's dysfunctional criminal justice system. There was a long and tedious wait ahead. Would we have to do it all over again in six months? Oh yes, we would!

27

DIRTY DEAL

After suffering decades of violent domestic terror followed by a campaign of gangland threats and shabby legal games, Jane Clarke had lost faith in justice being done. She knew, better than anyone that Frankie Donaldson would stop at nothing to cheat the system and grind her into the dirt. Jane had lost count of the number of times the Crown Office stated that Donaldson's trial would take place, only for his lawyers to conjure up yet more delays. Then, one day, it finally happened. Donaldson ran out of stunts, there were no more excuses and he had nowhere left to hide. An extraordinary 1,159 days after his arrest, Donaldson was forced to stand in the dock and admit being a bully who punches, chokes and terrorises women. So much for the reputation that causes knees to knock in the underworld.

Until that day, Jane believed he would never accept his guilt. In the end, he had a simple choice – either suffer the humiliation of every nasty detail of his brutality being played out in open court, which would almost certainly conclude with a guilty verdict, or seek to minimise the damage by sitting down behind closed doors in order to scratch out the best possible deal from the Crown. The spectre of the court hearing a terrified child's 999 call during one of Donaldson's explosions was probably a sobering factor in his decision to pick the latter option. As well as damage limitation, a guilty plea also maintained a vestige of power in Donaldson's hands – hugely important to a control freak.

The indictment contained 16 charges spanning 12 years. It alleged numerous acts of violence and threats against Jane, her sister Liz and a child. According to the painstakingly constructed police case, he punched, kicked and choked them, threatened to blow their heads off, rammed their car and used everyday items – car keys, dumbbells, a phone, a TV remote control – as weapons.

Yet despite abusing his wealth to contemptuously undermine and mock the courts and Crown for more than three years, he was still allowed to strike a favourable deal. Donaldson cherry-picked which charges to accept and which would be binned while also taking a red pen through some of the most toxic elements of those he admitted. The secretive plea bargain between Donaldson's lawyers and Crown prosecutors was appalling. The victims were never even told the full details of which charges were dropped or exactly how others had been amended. Only now, in this book, are the details being made public.

The Crown casually agreed to drop seven of the 16 charges, which meant that he pled guilty to nine. Of those, five were admitted in full, without any alterations. They were:

> Charge #1 – seizing Liz by the neck, dragging her to a front door, punching her face and then forcing her outside.

> Charge #6 – assaulting Jane by sitting astride her and injuring her by repeatedly hitting her head with a car key.

Charge #9 – injuring Jane by repeatedly punching her on the head and body.

Charge #11 – seizing Jane by the throat with both hands, pulling her out of bed onto the floor, holding her throat, punching her head and pulling her ears, causing injury.

Charge #13 – repeatedly punching Jane's head and body and repeatedly striking her head with a mobile phone and remote control, also causing injury.

While those five charges paint an unpleasant picture, the dropped and altered charges are more shocking still. Of the seven ditched by the Crown, three were relatively minor breaches of the peace but four were particularly lurid and varied in their nature. They were:

Charge #7 – alleging Donaldson assaulted a child, aged between eight and 12, by throwing and pushing him.

Charge #8 – chasing Jane and a child in a vehicle then ramming into it with his own. This was described as being like a scene from *Grand Theft Auto.*

Charge #12 – punching Jane, dragging her by the hair and repeatedly slamming her head against a car steering-wheel.

Charge #16 – threatening to shoot Jane and her family in the head, when they were dragged out of the panto, prompting his arrest in December 2013.

Just as galling as the dropped charges was the sleight of hand applied to four of Donaldson's nine guilty charges. His lawyer and the Crown conducted a process of sanitisation, softening or deleting the worst elements, often distorting their tone entirely.

Charge #3 concerned seizing Liz by the throat and threatening to throw her from a second-floor window. This was altered to say first floor, even though it happened in the second-floor flat of Jane and Liz's mother. Also deleted from this charge was the reference to pinning Liz *against* the window.

Charge #5 saw Donaldson admit hitting Jane on the body with a wet towel and wrapping it round her neck, restricting her breathing. But the Crown removed the word 'repeatedly' and that he had struck her head with it. Also excised was reference to the attack endangering her life.

Charge #15 was distorted beyond recognition. While Donaldson admitted assaulting Jane by pulling her body and striking her with a TV remote, the Crown deleted reference to him punching and kicking her head and body.

The most unpalatable amendment was to charge #14. Donaldson had been accused of repeatedly striking Jane on the head with a dumbbell, but this was removed, leaving a reference to throwing the dumbbell at her. Perhaps the Lord Advocate could then explain the permanent indentation in Jane's skull caused by the heavy weight crashing down upon her?

This was not justice but a gentleman's agreement carved out between a defence lawyer and a Crown prosecutor who ought to have known better. One justification for such deals is to give an accused person some benefit and reward for pleading guilty at an early stage, thereby saving court time and expense and reducing the distress of victims and witnesses. Clearly, Donaldson's three-year game of churn was the opposite of swift justice and victim consideration, and should, therefore, have precluded any goodwill from the Crown. Sadly, this was not a one-off but an example of Scotland's usually unseen, parallel justice, of clandestine pacts between lawyers.

Once the deal was rubber-stamped by Sheriff Joan Kerr, Crown prosecutor Harry Findlay provided a narrative of events which reflected the distorted indictment. The sheriff allowed Donaldson's bail to continue after hearing he had not breached the conditions since they were imposed.

Yet during those three long years of attrition, Jane and other witnesses had reported dozens of serious acts of intimidation, menacing texts and vandalism, including the threats to have acid thrown in her face at the school gates and for William 'Basil' Burns to shoot a child witness. At the time of writing, another Donaldson crony is still due to stand trial for allegedly threatening Jane and telling her to back off.

Clarke and her sister each submitted victim impact statements which set out the extent of their suffering and which the sheriff sees prior to passing sentence. Jane told the sheriff how Donaldson tried to control every aspect of her existence for years and how she only went to the police after he spent months bombarding her with threats and abuse while refusing to accept their relationship was over.

Much of Clarke's statement related to injuries she suffered. She wrote:

> It is very difficult to remember the amount of physical injuries I received during my 22 years with Frankie. I have three disfigurements on my face, two scars and one where a [dumbbell]

weight was used as a weapon. Throughout the years, the amount of one-off slaps and full-blown assaults are too many to be listed.

This obviously had a serious impact on my day-to-day life, causing me to change from an outgoing educated young woman into a frightened nervous wreck. I had to attend hospital, a psychologist and a counsellor to try and help me cope with my life. My mental health really deteriorated.

Talking about the detriment to her daily life and the nuclear option on the table of having to accept a new identity and life under the police's witness protection system, she wrote:

It is virtually impossible for anyone to understand the severity and ongoing torture I am subjected to. I have a [police] panic button, and cameras fitted where not even I know where the box is which constantly records. My only option is to enter into witness protection where I have been offered the full package. I think I have been isolated enough, however I still have to keep this option open.

As a qualified social worker, Jane has advised other women to leave abusive partners. She struggles to reconcile this with her own inability to do the same. She wrote:

The only way I could begin to describe or explain my situation is to say that I felt that I was in a cult. I felt brainwashed. I genuinely don't know who I was. I have been terrorised, left like a shaken, depressed and anxious woman. I am permanently anxious, I constantly risk-assess both me and my son's day-to-day survival. I don't ever believe I will return to the person I used to be but all I can hope for it that I can stay safe, sane and be a good mother.

Donaldson's guilty verdict was particularly poignant to the family of his former wife, Elaine Gemmill, who died of suspected suicide in 2003. Elaine had been forced to seek a court injunction banning Donaldson from coming anywhere near her. A criminal prosecution against Donaldson for domestic violence was unsuccessful, but the Gemmills have long known what domestic horrors Donaldson is capable of and blame him for Elaine's death at the age of 45. One family member, who asked not to be identified, told me: 'That bastard tortured Elaine for years. He put her in an early grave. Before her death, graffiti was put all over the outside of her house calling her a grass. He's nothing but a fucking rat and a dirty coward. Everyone is looking to see what sentence he gets. Look at the length of time it took to get done; it's a disgrace.'

The day after Elaine's body was found, Donaldson took their traumatised son, aged just 11, on a private jet to Seville to watch Celtic in the 2003 UEFA Cup Final.

Jane Clarke's ordeal has destroyed her faith in justice. Suffering years of terror, threats and uncertainty – only to be limply concluded with a cynical plea deal – has left her utterly disillusioned. One friend said, 'Jane feels that if she could rewind the clock, she would not have gone to the police. The cops who dealt with it were really professional and supportive, but once it reached the Crown, things started to go very badly wrong. The system is a shambles which someone like Donaldson can easily manipulate using his money and lawyers.'

Donaldson, displaying no outward trace of remorse, strutted out of court with an instruction to return for sentencing four weeks later. At least Jane hoped, if not fully believed, there could be no more game-playing, no more delays, no more hiding place for her tormentor. Donaldson was due to be sentenced on 30 March 2017 – exactly three years, three months and three days after he first appeared in the dock. That morning, the court was packed with those who wanted to see justice being done, but Donaldson had other plans and decided not to show up. His lawyer mumbled something about supposed ill health but produced no medical evidence to back up the claim. The sheriff shot down a request to delay sentencing for another six weeks and firmly told Donaldson's lawyer that his client had better be in front of her in one week's time, but did not issue an arrest warrant. Surely, next time, there could be no more delays? Surely Donaldson would finally be forced to take his punishment?

28

CALL CRIMESTOPPERS

I could hear a smile on the anonymous caller's face as he broke the news – Frankie Donaldson had been stabbed. A knifeman pounced as Donaldson was getting out of a car, 36 hours before he was due in court to be sentenced for the litany of assaults against Jane Clarke and her sister Liz. The caller said, 'He's in a bad way, he was hacked to bits. I was told they scalped him.'

Within five minutes came a different take from another caller, telling me: 'It's no more than a paper cut. I wouldn't be surprised if he arranged it himself just to avoid getting sentenced.'

As is so often the case with gangland rumours, neither of these early and conflicting analyses was entirely accurate. No, Donaldson's injuries were not serious, but neither was the attack self-inflicted.

The police issued a press release which did not identify the 58-year-old victim but stated that he had been 'specifically targeted'. The attack took place at 8.30 p.m. in a car park in Cumbernauld, 20 minutes north-east of Glasgow and one of numerous locations where Donaldson was known to spend nights, as he slipped nomadically between addresses. Detectives said the victim was 'seriously assaulted by a number of people' but were unable to say how many or provide a description of them or their vehicle, which 'would have been driven off at speed'.

I half expected a knock at the door from the police. More than one person, presumably in jest, asked me, 'You got an alibi?' Thankfully, I did.

With news of Donaldson's dramatic attack online and in the morning newspapers, no one expected that he would keep his date at Glasgow Sheriff Court. They were right. With Sheriff Joan Kerr on the bench, there was no sign of Donaldson. At least this time his lawyer had a decent excuse – and a sick note. The lawyer explained that his client had undergone unspecified surgery and was still in hospital, leaving the sheriff no option but to put justice on ice for another six weeks.

Jane's solicitor, Siobhán Kelly, wrote to prosecutor Harry Findlay raising concerns about the impact of the latest delay. The day after the no-show, Donaldson found the strength to clamber from his hospital bed and show face at the funeral of the ex-wife of his friend, Celtic director Michael McDonald. He was captured by a *Sunday Mail* photographer, his right hand enclosed in a cartoonish giant bandage, and a story was published with the headline 'FEELING A HOLE LOT BETTER, DONUTS?' That he is left-handed did not go unnoticed.

Perhaps the theory of Donaldson paying for a hit on himself was inspired by the recently released *T2 Trainspotting* movie in which another unhinged Francis – Franco Begbie – gets a prison pal to stick him with a blade in order to get out. Or maybe Donaldson was simply so petrified of jail that he would do anything to avoid it.

But why would he be so fearful of imprisonment? The answer lies in his deep unpopularity in the criminal underworld. Donaldson possesses the slippery skill to keep a foot in multiple and often rival camps, which can be seen as disloyalty and stir mistrust about whose side he is really on. More damaging still is the suspicion about how he has been able to thrive while many of his contemporaries have ended up poor, dead or in prison.

For all that Donaldson's blood boils at the derogatory 'Donuts' nickname, his other one – 'Crimestoppers' – is more uncomfortable. The police press release about the Cumbernauld stabbing included a plea for anyone with information about it to call the Crimestoppers phone number. This prompted his enemies to snort with knowing laughter – 'Call Crimestoppers about an attack on Crimestoppers!' Jane believes that her knowledge of some of Donaldson's secrets had been a factor in his decision to plead guilty rather than go to trial. She would have had no qualms about admitting making calls to Crimestoppers at Donaldson's behest while under his domestic subjugation.

With William 'Basil' Burns languishing on remand for the acid attack against me and the primary school shooting, he and his cronies were growing increasingly impatient with Donaldson. An impeccable source told me that the price for Burns attacking me was £30,000 – that was if the job was done correctly. I'm not sure exactly what outcome would have merited the full fee – blindness, disfigurement, death? That it was so badly executed meant that Burns had only got £10,000, leaving him muttering threats from his cell. There is no ombudsman for hitman pay disputes.

Burns had the backing of his closest friend, Robert 'Piggy' Pickett, a veteran of the 1990s Paisley drugs war with connections to the Lyons crime clan. Pickett is a dangerous and violent criminal who once went to jail rather than give evidence against two Daniel mob gunmen who shot him, but he is not an idiot. Pickett was smart enough to realise that going after a journalist was almost as stupid as targeting a police officer. I learned that he had been on holiday when the acid attack plot was hatched and put into action. Had he been at home, it simply would not have happened.

One source said, 'If Piggy had been around, he would have stopped Basil and you would not have been attacked. Basil is a rocket who would do anything for a few quid but Piggy would never have allowed it. He was raging when it happened, not just because his pal got jail, but because it was stupid and counter-productive.' It was a startling and sobering revelation that made me reflect on and almost admit the existence of an underworld moral code.

Donaldson had more than just Burns and Pickett to worry about. His influence also seeped into the long-running Daniel versus Lyons drugs war. At its peak in the late 2000s, against a raging backdrop of tit-for-tat shootings, Donaldson had a foot in both camps. Steven Lyons considered Donaldson to be a friend and ally and spent time with him socially. Lyons was therefore furious on discovering that Donaldson was also on civil terms with his most dangerous enemy – the Daniels' enforcer Kevin 'Gerbil' Carroll.

When the Lyons mobster Ross Monaghan stood trial for Carroll's Asda assassination, his lawyer theatrically read out a list of names of possible alternative suspects. The list of 99, compiled by police early on in the investigation, included Donaldson. It was a stunt designed to show the jury what kind of person Carroll was, but this who's who of gangland also serves to illustrate Donaldson's fluid loyalties.

In the weeks prior to Donaldson admitting the nine domestic violence charges, his name also cropped up in another murky incident which drew the ire of the Lyons *and* the Daniels. A major cocaine dealer and Carroll loyalist, who cannot be named for legal reasons, was arrested by armed police in a dramatic swoop in Rutherglen, just south of Glasgow. According to him, he had been lying low in a property linked to Donaldson and had been in his company shortly before the police pounced. The dealer and his Daniel cronies blamed Donaldson for the arrest. They are not the kind of people who believe in innocence until proven guilty – neither do they set any store by the requirement of proof beyond reasonable doubt. At least not in their own gangland version of justice. Unfortunately for Donaldson, the Lyons were equally sure of Donaldson's complicity and, on that basis, furious that the man had not been delivered to them instead of the police.

Another example of Donaldson's perceived disloyalty emerged after the murder of his brother-in-law, George 'Goofy' Docherty, a Paisley drugs war contemporary of Burns. Following his 2006 murder, Donaldson did not even attend his funeral. It was suggested the snub was because Donaldson was still harbouring ambitions that he could pass himself off as legitimate and therefore could not afford to soil his reputation by being seen at a gangland send-off. Even worse, Donaldson then committed what was viewed as great treachery by getting close to the very hitman suspected of getting away with killing Docherty.

Donaldson had long been conscious of the need to stay out of the spotlight which, in the age of social media, can be easier said than done. In 2015 I got a tip that a photo of Donaldson was on Facebook. Of particular interest was that he had his arm around a fresh-faced underworld hitman called Bobby Kirkwood. It was like an old football manager showing off his new star striker – all that was missing was the team scarf held aloft.

Kirkwood had come to public notoriety a few years earlier with an imaginative use of power tools in a particularly vicious attack. He was jailed for taking a power drill to gangster James Hanlon – another friend of the Daniels and Carroll. Kirkwood was one of the two men who growled at Jane Clarke after she arrived on a flight at Glasgow airport one day.

For years, Kirkwood's picture could not be published while Donaldson was facing trial for domestic violence. That meant he again enjoyed the protection of contempt of court laws which thwarted anyone telling the truth about his gangland connections while his case churned through court. Only now can we publish the photo but, as it was gathering digital dust, Kirkwood apparently decided he no longer wanted to play for Donaldson's team any more. Something to do with a lack of trust in him . . .

Another example of Donaldson's fickleness can be seen in his relationship with celebrity criminal Barry Hughes, which owes more to hard cash than matching star signs. Money is certainly persuasive enough for them all to quietly forget about an incident a decade earlier when Donaldson came close to a street clash with Hughes's father, Donald – a gangland version of a school reunion.

A more recent and particularly stark illustration of Donaldson's underworld ducking and diving emerged during a murder trial in March 2016. Drug-dealer Jamie 'Jamboy' Connelly ran up a £600 debt while working for a business which makes deliveries of alcohol to customers' homes. Business owner David 'Strathy' Strathern called on Donaldson to resolve the dispute. Donaldson set up a meeting between Strathern and Connelly at which the money would supposedly be repaid. The rendezvous took place in Rutherglen and ended with Connelly being stabbed to death. Prosecutor Tim Niven-Smith asked

Strathern, 'Frank Donaldson and [his associate] David Jones were the men who sorted out the dispute between you and Jamie and he was to pay you money?' Strathern replied, 'It was.'

The murder victim's father claimed the attack happened when Strathern got out of a car and lunged at his son, who lifted his shirt and said to his father, 'He got me a fucking cracker, Dad.' Strathern, who insisted Connelly was uninjured when he left and said he had no idea how he got the fatal stab wound, walked free courtesy of a not proven verdict.

So when Donaldson was stabbed and slashed in a Cumbernauld car park, the CID in Coatbridge would have been scratching their heads. Never mind a list of 99 suspects – it would have been more like 999. Theories were in abundance. The family of his first wife, Elaine Gemmill, were certainly not shedding any tears. Members of the Lyons and Daniel mobs were delighted but distanced themselves from the attack, with one stating, 'We'd have done it right.' The most compelling of the suggestions was that the stabbing was ordered by an old enemy from Glasgow's east end.

Back at court, Sheriff Kerr set a new date for sentencing – 19 May – which gave Donaldson six weeks to recover. When the day arrived, there were blue skies and sunshine so I decided to wait outside the court in order to have a word with Donaldson when he arrived. There were a few questions I intended to put to him. But it was yet another no-show.

When his lawyer flourished a psychiatric report which stated that he was too ill to stand trial, Sheriff Kerr pointed out that the report was invalid as this was a sentencing hearing, not a trial, and added, 'We have moved beyond that point.' She then told the lawyer in very clear terms that his wayward client had better turn up next time, on 6 June.

Meanwhile, Jane and her sister seethed impotently but they were used to it, having become numbed by years of incessant delays. They were certain that Donaldson would continue to find ways of dodging justice. His deep fear of jail might even make him jump on a plane to somewhere sunny for a very long holiday.

On 6 June I got a surprising message telling me that Donaldson was on his way to court. I still considered it to be unlikely and joked that he might end up steering his car into the River Clyde or deliberately fall down the court stairs. But at long last there he was, standing in the dock, nervous and sullen. Gone was the gallus self-styled businessman who had given a mocking performance during the civil case. Gone was the gangland fixer whose cash and connections made rivals quake.

It had been 16 years since I first wrote the story about the hitman plotting to 'put a hole in Donuts'. It had been four years since Jane flew home from Majorca with bleeding on the brain. It was three years and six months since his arrest in Glasgow following the threats that Jane and her family would be shot.

This, at long last, was the endgame. Donaldson had nothing to say for himself. His latest lawyer pleaded with the sheriff to spare him a prison sentence on the grounds that he was supposedly suffering from post-traumatic stress disorder and a cocaine habit. Apparently, the lawyer claimed, Donaldson was 'thoroughly ashamed of his behaviour', which were hollow and insulting words to his victims.

The sheriff listened to all the excuses, then said, 'I have reached the conclusion that the offences are so grave that no suitable alternative to a custodial sentence is possible.'

She told Donaldson that he was being sentenced to 26 months' imprisonment. Of course, he will serve nothing like that amount and the true duration of his sentence, as usual, will be kept from the public. In addition, the sheriff imposed a four-year order banning him from making contact with his battered, tormented and tortured ex, who had done what no man has ever done, which was to stand up to Donaldson and come out on top.

The agony for Jane was not over yet, though A month after being jailed, Donaldson again reached for the law and lodged an appeal against his sentence. The uncertainly hung over Jane for two more months until the appeal was rejected.

I spoke to Marsha Scott, chief executive of Scottish Women's Aid, who works with the police and Crown Office to improve the way the criminal justice system deals with domestic abuse. She and others in the charity have helped to achieve great progress over the years, but her assessment of this case – for which the maxim 'justice delayed is justice denied' could have been coined – was damning. She said:

> When a woman and her child have been so horrifically revictimised by the system that is supposed to protect them, then it is important that those within the system are asked, and indeed ask themselves, serious questions about how this came to be.
>
> It's hard to see this particular situation as anything but a catalogue of failures; failures that have let a woman and her child down. Despite improvements within the justice system, her [Jane Clarke's] story has shown that there is still a long way to go until women have equal access

to justice in Scotland. It is on all of those within
the system to reflect on how they can step up and
better protect victims of domestic abuse, and it is
on all of us to demand that they do.

I also talked to Donaldson's friend Colin McGowan,
chief executive of Hamilton Accies FC, who had given evidence on Donaldson's behalf during the failed civil case
against Jane. He expressed surprise at the violence and
compared the couple's relationship to that of 'Posh and
Becks'. In response to cocaine use being cited as an explanation of Donaldson's conduct, McGowan said, 'Frank's
wrestled with many demons over the years. Any form of
violence against anyone is wrong.'

The timing of Donaldson's imprisonment was pleas-
ingly significant, as it came the day after I returned to
the High Court for a re-run of the acid attack and school
shooting trial of his former friend William 'Basil' Burns.

29

THE LIE COURT

With the gaze of 15 fresh jurors directed towards me, I reminded myself that the criminal justice system is often seen as a game, and those who play it are sometimes willing to distort the truth in order to get the right result.

Life had been on resentful pause for six months following the collapse of the first trial due to the non-attendance at court of shooting victim and Daniel gang associate Ross Sherlock. When the second trial finally began at Glasgow's High Court in June 2017, I was again first up and Crown prosecutor Richard Goddard, moving at a quick pace, zipped through my account of the festive morning when the bogus postman came calling with a bottle of sulphuric acid. The same formulaic process followed. Point at William 'Basil' Burns in the dock. Examine items of evidence, including knife, acid bottle, Royal Mail jacket and bag. Describe photos of the scene as they appeared on big screens. When a gruesome image of my wounded feet was displayed for all to see, I grimaced. Poor jurors. 'Not your best side,' deadpanned the prosecutor. As before, I described my injuries, but this time just happened to recall that a small amount of acid splashed into my mouth, causing me to seek dental treatment days after the attack.

I steeled myself for another bout of verbal sparring with Thomas Ross, the lawyer hired to get Burns off the hook. The only positive from a re-match was the diminished likelihood of being ambushed. Gone was the initial shock-value as Ross served up the reheated defence centred on a fictional blackmail plot. While the accusations were just as nasty, they no longer had the sharp edge of surprise.

Ross also challenged the 'Wee Jamie sends his regards' comment muttered by Burns while being led away by police and suggested that I had orchestrated my neigh-bours' recollections of this being said. When I attempted to say that the 'Wee Jamie' comment was actually a red herring designed to throw me off the trail of the real puppet-master who paid Burns, I was steered back on track. The court was not interested in what facts I had since established and expected me to stay rigidly within the parameters of first-hand events.

During the first trial I had been asked by Ross about my 2006 phone call to Burns. In the second trial, the lawyer returned to the subject. On this occasion I was ready. I again admitted calling his client but this time explained why – Burns was in prison and I wanted to prove that he had an illicit mobile. I elaborated further, stating that the call featured in a *Sunday Mail* report about Frankie 'Donuts' Donaldson being vulnerable to gangland vultures due to the murder of his henchman George 'Goofy' Docherty and the long-term incarceration of Burns. However, my telling of this relevant and simple truth – that Burns had been in prison – was deemed unacceptable, possibly even unfair, to the grey man in the dock, and the jury was instructed to ignore it. The court wanted me to admit calling Burns but with no other context. By doing so, it would allow the defence to peddle the nonsense that my call was some kind of shakedown, an attempt to squeeze information from him against his will. This would then feed the bigger lie that I phoned Burns the night before the acid attack and threatened to blackmail him unless he told me about a particular murder.

Ross also put it to me that only Burns and I could know what had been said during the prison phone call 11 years earlier. Not so, I replied. Ross presumably did not expect me to reveal that I had retained the digital recording of the brief conversation which proved every single word of my version to be true. One imagines that in a US TV courtroom drama this would have elicited booms of 'Objection!' and heated debate about whether the tape could be introduced as evidence. But at the High Court it was as if I were speaking to myself and we ambled forwards without pause.

Prior to giving evidence, I had not learned the identity of the presiding judge and only afterwards discovered him to be Lord Matthews. The name rang a bell. I realised that I had written about him just a month before the acid attack. My light-hearted story told how he had accused police officers of being 'disrespectful' in their slovenly attire while giving evidence, with one being compared to Prohibition-era Chicago gangster Al Capone. While I was confident that the judge would not be unduly ruffled by our prior connection, thank goodness I had not turned up in a chalk-stripe suit and fedora.

The following day I scanned coverage of the trial on the BBC News website. With pleasing happenstance, the court report was placed immediately beside news of Donaldson's long overdue imprisonment for the campaign of violence and terror against Jane Clarke and her sister. The significance of this coincidence was understood by a handful of friends, journalist colleagues and, presumably, underworld inhabitants.

By day four of the trial, proceedings had reached the same point as day ten of the first one when they had come to an abrupt halt due to the AWOL Sherlock, who claimed to have fled Glasgow for London, apparently because the Lyons mob kept trying to shoot him. For his no-show, Sherlock was sent to prison. He argued that he should get bail but the Crown was having none of it. After his first disappearing act, there was no chance of them taking a risk. As it turned out, keeping him behind bars to guarantee his attendance almost backfired. Veteran *Daily Record* reporter Paul O'Hare revealed that Sherlock was slashed in the neck with a makeshift plastic blade following attendance at a church service inside Low Moss prison. According to gangland pundits, it was the sixth attempt on his life.

Sherlock's previous failure to turn up illustrated that he was completely unconcerned about justice being done and had absolutely no intention of implicating Burns. During his forced testimony, to no one's surprise, he crucially failed to identify Burns as the primary school shooter and neither, indeed, did any other Crown witness. As a consequence and also to no one's surprise – other than perhaps the Crown's – the judge ruled there was insufficient evidence to convict either Burns or Porter for the shooting, so they were duly acquitted.

Therefore, after 18 months of oppressive legal tedium and inaction, we were back to square one. It gave me no satisfaction to see the charge dropped but it supported my belief that running the acid attack and school shooting trials in tandem was cynical, opportunistic and destined to be fruitless. If anything, it put the acid attack prosecution at risk of failure by dragging out proceedings and forcing Burns and his lawyer to cook up their wild defence, which they might not have done had they faced the single acid attack charge – one to which they could have discreetly wangled a favourable guilty plea deal.

There were two questions I kept asking myself. Why did the Crown not prosecute Burns for the acid attack alone, given his overwhelmingly obvious guilt? Why risk jeopardising that slam-dunk conviction by hitching it to a seedy Daniel versus Lyons gangland shooting for which there was virtually zero evidence? As I put it in my plea to the Lord Advocate following the collapse of the first trial: 'The non-attendance of Mr Sherlock in itself should be reason enough to prosecute my crime separately, and to do so timeously.'

Burns, a veteran of lying under oath in his own defence, was up next. I braced myself. He did not disappoint, and it was perhaps a blessing that I was not present as I would have caused a distraction either by uncontrollable chuckling or steam coming from my ears.

Burns began by telling the jurors that I was 'incapable of telling the truth about anything' before he spun them a very carefully constructed web of lies. As anticipated, he claimed that I had phoned him the night before the attack to demand information about a murder victim, with me threatening to share compromising photos of him with 'a young blonde woman'. According to his script, Burns then signed off with a threat to pay me a visit – to which I laughingly responded that he did not know where I lived. Undeterred, Burns claimed he left Paisley at 7 a.m., took two buses to the west end of Glasgow and then walked along random streets hunting for my car. Miraculously, he discovered it on the fourth street he tried. What are the chances?

He also had an explanation for his unorthodox Royal Mail garb. The postman's uniform was worn in order to disguise himself from me as I knew what he looked like

– even though I did not. As the yarn continued, it did not get any less bold. Burns claimed that he barged through my front door with the intention of assaulting me but, from the shadows, a mystery man appeared and knocked him unconscious. When Burns came round, I was on top of him with a knife levelled at his throat. With a straight face, he told the jurors, 'Russell Findlay was scraping a knife across my face. He said, "Don't fucking move, Basil boy, or you're getting it right through your neck."' I then stabbed his chin, hence the four stitches he received – although that injury was actually caused by me punching him. With a dash of mystery, he added, 'I think they were waiting for me.' The 'Wee Jamie sends his regards' comment was denied by Burns. He explained that this was not the kind of fancy talk used on the mean streets of Paisley. This was labelled the 'Ferguslie Park defence' by one bemused observer.

Then came his climactic *pièce de résistance*. Bidding a final farewell to the last shred of his reputation as one of Scotland's most feared underworld hitmen, Burns denied throwing the sulphuric acid in my face. Therefore I must have done so myself. Goddard said, 'What you are saying is absolutely preposterous' – to which Burns mumbled, 'No it's not.'

In his closing speech, Ross told the jurors to be wary of my evidence, saying, 'He said that acid actually went into his mouth. That was a barefaced lie. A doctor who examined him checked his mouth and said there was zero evidence of damage.'

When I read these words, I was outraged. Medical evidence of the acid going into my mouth was available to the police and the prosecution. My dental appointment to examine the acid damage to the enamel on my teeth was a matter of indisputable record. The prosecution had not led this evidence, simply because it was not considered to be of any great significance. But the innocent omission of it from the prosecution case most certainly did not prove, as Ross contested, that I had told a 'barefaced lie'.

Another claim Ross made during his closing speech caused me to bristle. He said, 'Mr Findlay is a journalist and an author and is likely making money out of this.' Did I understand that correctly? A dangerous criminal had invaded my family home in order to maim or kill me, yet his lawyer was suggesting that this was actually a golden opportunity for me to make a quick buck.

A quick scan of the accounts of the Scottish Legal Aid Board told me that only one person was getting rich on the back of this crime, and it certainly was not me. Over the last five-year period, Ross received £932,000 for representing accused criminals. The most recently available accounts state that he relieved £239,000 from taxpayers in a single year (almost enough to pay the salaries of ten new police officers). I later established that Ross received more than £19,000 to defend Burns. The cost to the public purse is another reminder of the reality of legal aid largesse, despite the profession's incessant protestations to the contrary.

After just over three weeks, the trial drew to a close on 26 June 2017. I had gone on holiday two days earlier, with the lies and smears crowding my thoughts. All I could do was hope that the good Glaswegian jurors did not believe in conspiracy theories.

30

DEAD GUILTY

The prisoner put on a suit and a shirt and tie before being handcuffed and escorted by guards into a high-security van for the short rush-hour commute to court. Then, as William 'Basil' Burns took his seat in the dock beside co-accused Alex Porter, the cuffs were removed, and by the time the jurors filed in for another day of civic duty he had become a study of unremarkable neutrality, a grey man who did not merit a second glance.

Human alchemy, from snarling Paisley gangster Basil who glories in amoral violence to Mr Burns, 'the accused' with a right of presumed innocence, took place every morning for three weeks. The jury of ten women and five men sat in respectful silence as the prosecution of Burns and Porter played out. It was simple truth versus towering lies. In the end, Burns could drop his act. The game was up. Not a single juror was taken in by his practised routine, his ludicrous testimony of fictitious blackmail plots or his defence lawyer's calculated tactic of smearing me, the innocent victim.

Once the jury delivered their unanimous guilty verdict, Burns could stop pretending, regress to his persona of Basil, go back to jail and remove his crumpled suit. It would be another month before Lord Matthews was ready to pass sentence.

It took the criminal justice system 18 months to arrive at this point, for Burns to be convicted of throwing sulphuric acid in my face 'to the endangerment' of my life. A great deal of time, huge financial cost and immeasurable disruption to many people's lives, in order to secure this, the easiest of convictions – of a ludicrous hitman in fancy dress caught red-handed at the scene of the crime. No wonder the Crown Office flaps, flails and surrenders in the pursuit of cases considered complex or challenging. When I heard the outcome, the sensation of relief was overwhelming. Logic told me that the jury could not possibly be hoodwinked, but at the back of my mind had been a tiny, incessant whisper of uneasy doubt.

While I viewed his co-accused Porter as being equally guilty, the evidence was so thin I was unsurprised when he walked free, his charges not proven. Prior to the second trial I had established that Porter had obtained from an unwitting Paisley postie the Royal Mail uniform used by Burns. He also acquired the steak knife which carried his DNA. Police found five out of a set of six in his partner's home. I was certain Porter was the getaway driver and fully cognisant of the dark nature of the mission to my home. When he was found dead 12 days later, I shrugged. It was suggested that Porter took his own life because he could no longer cope with the unbearable pressure to say and do what was ordered by his crime masters.

It was just before noon in Scotland when the verdict came and I was on holiday in Tokyo, where it was nearing 8 p.m. During the evening and into the night I remained wide-eyed in the darkness as a slew of messages arrived from daytime Scotland, travelling over 9,000 miles in a digital heartbeat. I mischievously tweeted a cartoon I had drawn of a ruddy-faced lawyer, a puppet of organised crime, studying a book titled *Fairy Tales for Defence Spivs*.

Reports of the outcome generated a fresh deluge of goodwill and voices from the past, just as had happened when news of the attack first circulated.

The police released a mugshot of Burns. He should be grateful they withheld the photo taken after his arrest when his face was battered, bruised, swollen and stitched. Detective Sergeant Craig Warren issued a statement, describing Burns as a 'career criminal' with links to serious organised crime. He added, 'This was a vicious assault which took place in broad daylight, and shows the sheer contempt that he had for Mr Findlay and his young daughter.'

If any of the jurors had any lingering doubt about their decision, they would surely have been dispelled when they heard Burns's sordid record, not least shooting an innocent woman during an armed robbery and the theft of a birthday cake at gunpoint. They would not have been told about his acquittal for the 1994 gun murder of 23-year-old Raymond McCafferty in Carnwadric, Glasgow – the £2,000 hit that sealed his reputation as a go-to thug for hire.

Also passing unnoticed was the interesting alibi Burns had come up with for the shooting of Ross Sherlock. At the moment Sherlock was gunned down outside a primary school, Burns claimed he was working at sprawling tyre-recycling plant Guinea Enviro in Glasgow's Maryhill. Two years previously, I had investigated this business and found that it was run by gangster Steven Scott, who had just served time for gun possession. The published story stated that Scott had links to a 'multi-millionaire Mr Big'. What could not be stated was that Scott's mystery associate was gangland's bad penny, Frankie 'Donuts' Donaldson. Donaldson's name had been omitted from my newspaper story because of the contempt of court law which inadvertently shielded him while he spent years churning his domestic violence case.

The acid attack verdict came during an explosive revival of the long-running feud between the Daniel and Lyons families, with their various fluid factions and offshoots reaching out from north Glasgow housing estates to communities across the country, from Greenock in the west and Edinburgh in the east. The most recent re-ignition happened in January 2017, when the Lyons clan member Ross Monaghan was shot outside a south Glasgow primary school. This became the first of seven high-profile attacks that year, although many more went unreported by the newspapers.

The following month, the home of Francis 'Fraggle' Green, a son of late crime boss Jamie Daniel, was hit with gunfire. Soon after came the blade attack on Sherlock while he was leaving a prison chapel.

Within a few more weeks, another senior Daniel figure was targeted in a drive-by shooting. Robert Daniel was in a car outside his home in Stepps, near Glasgow, when a volley of shots was unleashed from a vehicle. He was hit but survived.

Next was Steven 'Bonzo' Daniel, who was driving a discreet private hire taxi, which was chased at high speed by two other vehicles, then rammed off the road. So severe were the subsequent knife wounds to Bonzo's face that his teeth and jawbone were exposed and the police initially mistook his injuries for a shooting.

It was then the turn of Craig 'Rob Roy' Gallagher, who has flipped between both sides and who I had first unmasked five years earlier. Gallagher was a partner in crime of Daniel enforcer Kevin 'Gerbil' Carroll – his 'alien abduction' sidekick – and he was arrested, albeit not prosecuted, for his murder. In July 2017 Gallagher was stabbed and tortured and, somehow, ended up being set on fire before managing to flee from a disused house in New Stevenston, Lanarkshire. It is unclear whether his captors torched him or whether he did it himself.

The most recent reported incident in this fresh blood-letting had a direct connection to Burns. As the suspected shooter of Sherlock, Burns was a prominent name on the Daniels' hit list. While in prison, Jamie Daniel Jr, a brother of Robert Daniel, had been trying to elicit information about Burns – where he was, who could get close to him, how best he could be harmed – but he must have asked the wrong people. The result of Jamie Jr's clumsy intelligence gathering efforts was that the tables were turned and he became the target. A Lyons mob thug is one of four men considered responsible for the subsequent, non-fatal blade attack on Jamie Jr, who was stabbed and slashed in Milton, Glasgow.

The new outbreak compelled Police Scotland, some broadsheet newspapers and some broadcasters to cautiously suggest to the nation the possible existence of an underworld feud between two rival groups. This was not news – it was the journalistic equivalent of reporting Third Lanark's football results.

The police were even moved to announce the creation of a specialist unit to 'dismantle' the criminal networks of the Daniels and Lyons, including their money-laundering front businesses where millions of pounds of dirty cash are magicked into seemingly legitimate income and assets.

It is possible that the police were being sincere but, even allowing for the impediment of gangland *omertà*, they have already had many long years in which to act. It is therefore tempting to view their tough talk as a cynical example of policing by PR – just something designed to alleviate public concerns about middle-aged morons risking the lives of innocent children by taking pot-shots at each other outside primary schools.

And so it continues. Each of these acts of extreme violence spanning the first seven months of 2017 was typically cowardly and vile. When it does inevitably diminish, it will be because money talks. Wise heads on each side will prevail by pointing out the negative impact these atrocities have on their vast drug-dealing profits. But once peace returns, will it be permanent?

31

NUMBERS GAME

Fifteen years is a long time to be locked up. That, according to what Scotland's judicial authorities told the public, was the weighty sentence imposed on William 'Basil' Burns for his well planned but poorly executed acid attack on me.

I was too busy to attend court, as tempting as it was to wave farewell to my hitman, and learned of the 'extended sentence of 15 years' from the official Twitter account of the Judicial Office for Scotland. Being familiar with sentencing opacity, I was wary. I studied a linked 500-word statement by Lord Matthews and found what I was looking for in the second last paragraph, which stated, 'That sentence will be in two parts and will run from 30 July 2016. The first part, the custodial element, will be ten years imprisonment. The second part, or extension period, will be five years.' OK, clearly not 15 years then. Still confused by the ambiguity, I asked the Crown Office, 'Would Burns therefore serve a full ten-year prison term?' Back came the explanation: 'It is my understanding that he would be eligible to apply for parole (no guarantee he will get parole) before he has served the full ten years. When he is released he would then be monitored for a period of five years.' The Crown official added that if I wanted to know any more, then I needed to fill out some forms issued by the Scottish Prison Service. These arrived several months later, after my second request for them. What better way to frustrate crime victims than with red tape?

I dug deeper. My research found that Burns will actually be eligible to apply for parole after serving just half his prison sentence. The rules used to be that it was two thirds. So with Burns's sentence being backdated for time spent on remand, that means he could be set free as early as summer 2021 – just *four years* after being sent down by Lord Matthews and in stark contrast to the 15 years tweeted by a judicial PR flunkey.

The decision to routinely dupe the public over sentencing owes much to the disconnect between people's expectation of lengthy prison terms for serious criminals and the collective touchy-feely ethos of liberal politicians, wet social workers and obedient prosecutors dancing to the politicians' tunes. What is harder to understand is judges' apparent willingness to go along with the mass exercise in deceit.

Burns must have been beaming with glee, although such good fortune was not entirely novel. I found a 2001 court report when Lord Penrose sentenced him for shooting a woman during an armed robbery. The judge said the crime was of such gravity that he considered giving Burns a life sentence. Instead, just like Lord Matthews, he gave him 15 years. Except, as we know, Burns was released early twice during that 15-year sentence and should have been locked up on the day he hurled acid in my face and set out to stab me.

In many countries, parole decisions are a transparent and routine part of the justice process, but in Scotland the public have no right to know how long a convict actually serves. Other than life sentences, which stipulate a minimum time behind bars, the numbers parroted by sheriffs and judges are illusory.

The power to free prisoners is in the gift of the Parole Board for Scotland, which is dominated by social workers, solicitors and others of that ilk. Volatile and violent people are routinely and prematurely released. In an era of increasing transparency, it is puzzling that casual misrepresentation, public endangerment and secrecy should be so readily accepted. Society seems to have a quaintly paternalistic trust that the board knows best. Even when these officials commit gross misjudgements, as they did by twice releasing Burns, they face no consequences due to politicians and the media being oddly incurious about explanations. Had Burns stuck me fatally with his knife, would parole officials been compelled to justify his early release? I assume not.

For Burns, it seemed that sentencing could not have come at a worse moment, as Britain was experiencing a spike in the number of high-profile attacks in which corrosive substances are used to maim, blind and disfigure. While such attacks may have their roots in so-called honour crimes, with women punished for disobeying cultural norms, it is evident that they have spread into the criminal underworld and, more worryingly still, the mainstream of school playgrounds, nightclubs and high streets. Hardly a day passes without news of yet another horror attack or a scarred victim stepping forward to publicly demand action from politicians and the justice system.

Over a period of 90 minutes during one weekend in July 2017, a spate of acid attacks in London pushed the issue to the forefront of the news and political agenda. Five fast-food delivery drivers – innocent workers out earning a modest wage – were struck in the faces with toxic substances in an alleged attempt to rob them. One suffered life-changing injuries. This sickening spree prompted a sea change with Conservative Home Secretary Amber Rudd suggesting that 'life sentences' be imposed on perpetrators, while Labour MP Stephen Timms led a debate in the House of Commons with demands that the sale of such substances should be strictly controlled and their public possession should be outlawed just like knives and guns.

Burns was the first high-profile acid attacker to be sentenced in the wake of this clamour. While criminal justice is a devolved matter for the Scottish government, the widespread UK media coverage brought extra attention to his sentencing. Stig Abell, a broadcaster and editor of the *Times Literary Supplement*, amusingly tweeted, 'Man threw acid in journalist's face; journalist knocked him down until cops came. They make them tough in Scotland.'

Lord Matthews could not allow the wall of political and media noise to influence his decision. Even so, Burns got off lightly with his '15 years'. The taste in my mouth was more bitter and longer lasting than that of the sulphuric acid.

I chose not to complete a 'victim impact statement', which allows victims to explain how a crime has affected them, because to do so was pointless. These were heralded as giving a voice to victims but, as they cannot influence a judge's sentencing decision, they are virtually meaningless. It is unfortunate that MSPs regard such gesture politics as an achievement.

Lord Matthews made some welcome points in his speech to Burns, describing the evidence against him as 'overwhelming' and his testimony 'an obvious fabrication from start to finish'. Speaking directly to Burns in the dock, the judge continued:

You went to his house in the morning, disguised as a postman, and threw acid at him with the plain intention of causing him severe damage. The evidence showed that you were also armed with a knife but thankfully you did not get the chance to use it.

To some extent you bit off more than you could chew. Mr Findlay did not take your attack lying down. He was able to overpower you and with the prompt assistance of neighbours you were detained there and then. Due to the intervention of those neighbours, Mr Findlay's injuries were not as bad as they might have been.

It is or should be well known that acid has the potential to cause catastrophic damage and it is no thanks to you that that was not the case here.

He then turned to the subject of Burns's motive, surmising that 'the only reason I can discern for your actions is that you objected to something that your victim wrote', before adding, 'The freedom of the press is an essential tool in the armoury of any democracy and attacks of this nature will not be tolerated.' On balance, this perception was preferable for Burns, rather than the truth that he was a mercenary thug in the pay of organised crime, but I did not want mistruth about his motive taking hold.

Since my defiant tweet about a 'fat hitman' leaving his broken false teeth in my driveway, sent hours after the attack, I had remained mute. While live court proceedings prohibited me from saying anything meaningful, I was aware of nonsense rumours – including one suggesting Jamie Daniel had ordered the attack. I was glad also to nail these lies while also being free to question why the police and Crown had no apparent desire to discover who had hired Burns.

My phone began to ring with broadcast and newspaper journalists seeking my views. I was happy to oblige, although I was also cautious about being perceived as the type of 'journalist' whose job is to opine – the newsprint version of a droning old golf club bore. The journalism trade publication *Press Gazette* ran an article about the sentencing, which included the judge's comment about Burns's being driven to attack me by something I had written. In response, I said:

> While journalists should welcome the points made by Lord Matthews about the importance of press freedom, speculation that Burns may have been motivated by something I wrote is wide of the mark. Following the attack, I quickly established that Burns was a paid hitman, hired by a very wealthy organised criminal who has been the subject of numerous stories by me. However, neither Police Scotland nor the Crown Office has shown any inclination to bring this man to justice.
>
> Their apparent disinterest may stem from the fact I was not killed or seriously hurt and that the paymaster is now serving a prison sentence for another, unrelated matter.
>
> However, it is imperative that a proper investigation takes place. A message should be sent to organised crime in the UK that attacks on journalists will not be tolerated. For the authorities to sit on their hands sets a very dangerous precedent.

I was under no illusion that my public tuppenceworth would have any effect on the police or Crown. As far as they were concerned, the conviction of Burns was job done. Who paid him? Who cares? I was easy to ignore. While my contribution to the debate was never likely to achieve anything tangible, at least it gave me some free therapy.

I was targeted because of my job, which is to go after powerful and wealthy people – be they gangsters, police officers, lawyers, judges or politicians – who think the rules don't apply to them. Journalism has suffered a bad press in recent years, but some of its most shrill critics are cursed with bovine ignorance. Without robust, aggressive and determined journalists and a buoyant industry which refuses to be neutered by the state, we would live in a much darker place.

While acid attacks are an important issue, of greater importance still is the cancer of domestic abuse. My attack was a by-product of the terror campaign inflicted on Jane Clarke. The choice of acid as weapon was incidental. Her appalling experience shows that, despite years of political rhetoric, domestic violence victims can still be treated with disdain by a justice system which will never change while Scotland's legal establishment is allowed to protect its vested interests. Jane has no faith in the police being able to protect her when Frankie 'Donuts' Donaldson is freed.

I take comfort that both Burns and Donaldson ended up behind bars. It amused me when the prison authorities kept them apart over concerns for their safety and Donaldson sought safe refuge in a wing for elderly prisoners. It felt like karma when he suffered a second blade attack, this time in the gym at Low Moss prison, less than three months into his sentence. Every day, I take even greater comfort from being able to recognise my face in the mirror, unlike other poor souls who have suffered devastating damage, physical and psychological, from acid attacks.

AUTHOR'S NOTE

My acid attack was rooted in the domestic violence and abuse perpetrated for years by a dangerous criminal against his long-term partner and her family. A few weeks before justice finally caught up with Frankie Donaldson and he was jailed for domestic violence, a new Bill was introduced to the Scottish Parliament. It is likely to pass into law in 2018 or 2019 and is expected to create a specific criminal offence of 'abusive behaviour', including psychological abuse such as coercion and control.

The new law is welcome. But it is vital that abusers are no longer allowed to use the criminal justice system as a weapon against their victims, and that prosecutors and judges end the entrenched culture of delays in the legal process which causes so much additional and unnecessary suffering.

Anyone with experience of domestic abuse who requires support can call the free and confidential helpline which is open 24 hours every day: 0800 027 1234.

Also available by Russell Findlay

Caught in the Crossfire
Scotland's Deadliest Drugs War

Scotland's deadliest gang war for a generation – the Daniel family versus the Lyons – was sparked by a cocaine theft from a house party which unleashed a decade of murderous violence. Devastation ensued . . . beatings, slashings, abductions and torture. Homes were firebombed while children slept; witnesses were forced into protection and families ripped apart. Michael Lyons, 21, was slaughtered with British Army guns in a triple shooting at a north Glasgow garage. Daniel enforcer Kevin 'Gerbil' Carroll, 29, had 13 shots pumped into him outside an Asda supermarket. The desecration of the grave of eight-year-old cancer victim Garry Lyons marked a sickening low.

Caught in the crossfire were brave parents in Milton, Glasgow, who opposed their community centre being used as a taxpayer-funded gang hut by the Lyons. Against the odds, they won their six-year battle which exposed a murky nexus between police officers, politicians and the underworld. This is the explosive story of how the Daniel–Lyons feud engulfed a community and spread from the mean streets into the corridors of power.

'Without [Russell Findlay of] the *Sunday Mail* exposing what was going on in Chirnsyde, it would have disappeared from the public eye.'

Sandra White MSP

The Iceman
The Rise and Fall of a Crime Lord

(with Jim Wilson)

The elite police officers secretly launching Scotland's biggest ever offensive against organised crime had only one target. His name was Jamie Stevenson but he was known as The Iceman, the biggest drugs trafficker the country has ever seen.

Suspected of a string of murders – including the gangland assassination of his best friend – Stevenson's decade-long rise was built on ruthless ambition, strategic cunning and calculated, brutal violence. It left him at the head of one of Europe's biggest smuggling operations pouring tons of drugs and guns onto the streets of Scotland

The Iceman tells the astonishing story of Stevenson's rise and fall, offering a unique and explosive insight into Operation Folklore, the unprecedented four-year investigation that ended in his arrest. It lays bare the blood-soaked business of Scotland's most powerful crime lord and, for the first time, exposes how Stevenson made – and laundered – his dirty millions.

'Unflinching . . . punchily written'   *The Herald*